*The Secret Life of John C. Van Dyke*

# *The Secret Life of John C. Van Dyke*

## SELECTED LETTERS

EDITED, WITH AN INTRODUCTION BY
David W. Teague and Peter Wild

University of Nevada Press
Reno • Las Vegas

WESTERN LITERATURE SERIES

University of Nevada Press, Reno, Nevada 89557 USA

Manufactured in the United States of America
Book design by Carrie Nelson House
Library of Congress Cataloging-in-Publication Data
Van Dyke, John Charles, 1856–1932.
The secret life of John C. Van Dyke : selected letters / edited, with an introduction by David W. Teague and Peter Wild.
p. cm. — (Western literature series)
Includes bibliographical references and index.
ISBN 0-87417-294-2 (alk. paper)
1. Van Dyke, John Charles, 1856–1932. Desert. 2. Deserts—Southwest, New. 3. Natural history—Southwest, New. 4. Natural history—Sonoran Desert. 5. Southwest, New—Description and travel. 6. Sonoran Desert—Description and travel. 7. Van Dyke, John Charles, 1856–1932—Correspondence. 8. Art historians—United States—Correspondence. 9. Naturalists—West (U.S.)—Correspondence. I. Teague, David W. (David Warfield), 1964– II. Wild, Peter, 1940– . III. Title. IV. Series.
F786.V24 1997 96-49496
973.91—dc21 CIP
The paper used in this book meets the requirements of American National Standard for Information Sciences—Permanence of Paper for Printed Library Materials, ANSI Z39.48-1984. Binding materials were selected for strength and durability.

First Printing

06 05 04 03 02 01 00 99 98 97 5 4 3 2 1

*Unless otherwise credited, all illustrations are courtesy of the Gardner A. Sage Library, New Brunswick Theological Seminary.*

*Frontispiece: This portrait of John C. Van Dyke at thirty was painted by William Merritt Chase, one of the preeminent artists of the American* fin de siècle. *The oil hangs in the Gardner A. Sage Library of the New Brunswick Theological Seminary.*

*For my grandparents, Milton and Ethel Teague,*
*who always had faith.*

DAVID TEAGUE

*For my parents, once again.*

PETER WILD

# *Contents*

# *Acknowledgments*

Many people helped shape this book. Leading the list are librarians: Renée S. House, director of the Gardner A. Sage Library of the New Brunswick Theological Seminary; Nancy Johnson and her assistant, Kathryn Talalay, at the American Academy of Arts and Letters; Lois Olsrud, Ruth H. Dickstein, Teresa Salazar, Louis Hieb, Roger Myers, and Peter Steere, all of the University of Arizona Library. Friends with various specialties also guided us through problems to solutions: Carl Berkhout, Germaine L. Moon, Dennis G. Casebier, Donald A. Barclay, James H. Maguire, and Neil Carmony. We thank Leonardo Varela Espinosa and Alberto Búrquez for their splendid research in Mexico's unknown places and David Yetman who brought us together; and Joyce García for her swift and accurate transformations of Spanish documents into English.

We appreciate the early encouragement of Joseph Wilder, editor of *Journal of the Southwest.* Some of the following letters first appeared in the *Journal* under the title "The Secret Life of John C. Van Dyke: Decalcomania on the Desert."

We thank Jay Paul Minn, translator of Pierre Loti's *Le Désert*, for rendering the Loti letter below into English.

Laura Howard worked smoothly and independently as a researcher, and once again Peggy Flyntz proved invaluable with her editorial assistance.

For their gracious help and for their kind permission to reprint the letters below from their holdings, we thank the following: Alan Van Dyke Golden; the Alexander Library, Rutgers University; the American Academy of Arts and Letters, New York City; the Arizona Historical Society; the Avery Architectural and Fine Arts Library, Columbia University in the City of New York; The *Barstow Desert Dispatch;* the Butler Library, Columbia University in the City of New York; Charles Scribner's Sons Archives; the Library of Congress; the New York Public Library; the New Brunswick Theological Seminary Archives, Gardner A. Sage Library; the Newberry Library; Princeton University Libraries; the Smithsonian Institution; and the Southwest Museum.

# *Introduction*

Few cultural changes in America are as easily pinpointed as the radical shift in attitudes toward the Southwest's deserts. The pivotal date was 1901, the year John C. Van Dyke (1856–1932) published *The Desert.* Though as early as 1863 traveler J. Ross Browne was singing about "a glowing and mystic land," his words hardly were typical of earnest settlers slogging through the nearly waterless sands toward California (47). Along with most pioneers, the utilitarian nation despised deserts as "God's mistakes," as wastelands. Yet attitudes changed over the decades, and Van Dyke's *The Desert* marked the culmination of a huge swing from traditional scorn to viewing the Southwest as a region to be appreciated for its wild beauty. So essential was the volume's role in confirming the cultural shift that Lawrence Clark Powell declares, "All Southwestern book trails lead to *The Desert*" (315), and that modern-day icon of desert lovers, Edward Abbey's *Desert Solitaire*, puts *The Desert* on the short list of essential reading (239).

As with most cultural changes, complexities lay behind the book's effectiveness. For one thing, long before Van Dyke arrived, prospectors had found gold out there. The millions of dollars' worth of ore eagerly dug from the sands and blasted from the rock helped launch the growing enthusiasm for the desert as a dawnland, a profitable phantasm. Tuberculars had discovered different treasures. Not only did the dry desert climate pull many of them back from a miserable, hacking death, they watched in amazement as vegetative profusions spurted from the sands—oranges, pomegranates, dates, and other fruits formerly known only in Sinbad tales. On top of that, by the turn of the century, deserts were no longer the genuinely fearsome places they had once been for settlers of European descent. By then, the Apaches and other tribes had been bludgeoned into submission, and railroads made travel through the region relatively easy. Dovetailing nicely with this were more favorable sentiments toward nature occurring when a recently industrialized people, turning romantic, now idealized the wilderness it had just conquered. In this, the fact that the desert was a new landscape, far different from the rest of the Republic, played to the region's favor. Romantics thrive on exoticism. The strange scenery of lava peaks and endless cactus flats, together with the unusual animals and native peoples, quickly caught the fancy of travelers, armchair and otherwise, from the staid eastern seaboard.[1]

Old prejudices die hard, but Van Dyke's *The Desert* clinched the issue by opening the eyes of the American masses to the new appreciation. Praising the arid lands for their forms and colors, this forceful and poetic work turned the old prejudices inside out and gave focus to the positive sentiments already in the making. For instance, Van Dyke on sand dunes:

> The long line of dunes at the north are just as desolate, yet they are wonderfully beautiful. The desert sand is finer than snow, and its curves and arches, as it builds its succession of drifts out and over an arroyo, are as graceful as the lines of running water. The dunes are always rhythmical and flowing in their forms; and for color the desert has nothing that surpasses them. In the early morning, before the sun is up, they are air-blue, reflecting the sky overhead; . . . under a blue moonlight they shine white as icebergs in the northern seas. (53)

With such emotional surges, Van Dyke offered Americans an aesthetic vocabulary to address the new region.

All to the better for the book's success, Van Dyke himself fit the role of the Byronic hero. Strapping on his pistol, Van Dyke swung his leg over his Indian pony and rode off into the unknown. As he went, he hailed his city-bound readers back East, urging them to ride with him "over the enchanted mesas of Arizona" and "beyond the wire fence of civilization" into a land of howling wolves and lurking bandits (x). He was just the sort of heroic figure needed for an urbanizing age having self-doubts about its own outdoor vigor and yearning to believe that such wild places as Van Dyke described still existed. With the heady assurances of *The Desert*, the nation trembled collectively with a pleasurable *frisson.*

As effective as the little book was, launching the now-popular genre of desert writing, we are beginning to understand that things were not always as Van Dyke represented them. As intimated above, by the time Van Dyke arrived, the Southwest hardly was the wild place he described. His Southwest was a wild place of the imagination deftly turned to literary advantage. Further,

Van Dyke hardly was the man he made himself out to be, one who possessed, besides high literary skill, an impressive frontier savvy and derring-do. Contrary to his myth, Van Dyke was a refined and wealthy patrician from an old and politically powerful family of New Brunswick, New Jersey. Over the years earning an enviable reputation as one of the nation's foremost Rembrandt scholars, he also turned his boundless energy and many-sided talents into dozens of popular books on art, travel, and nature. The first professor of art history at Rutgers University, he also served concurrently as the director of the equally prestigious Gardner A. Sage Library of the New Brunswick Theological Seminary. Conveniently, this was just across the street from Rutgers and up on what is known to this day as "Holy Hill." To top things off, art critic Van Dyke was hardly a two-fisted wanderer. He likely saw the Southwest through the windows of Pullman cars and from the verandahs of first-class hotels (Wild and Carmony).

In other words, in simplest terms Van Dyke did what many a successful writer does: he gave his readers the fantasy world they yearned for. Van Dyke's fantasy desert of chromatic colors and enchanting distances still holds sway with the public, as healthy sales for *The Desert*, even after nearly a hundred years, bear witness.

However, things rarely are as simple as they seem. To emphasize the public's gullibility by pointing to the literary jugglery of *The Desert* and leave it at that hardly is worth the while, given any number of fine books throughout history spun from fantasy and represented as fact. And neither is it edifying in itself to enumerate Van Dyke's tricks in projecting a false public image. Such, too, hardly is unusual with culture heroes. The issue, rather, is this: we are only now learning how extremely different a man Van Dyke was from what we thought, and these extreme differences determined the shape of the most influential book ever written about America's arid lands. For the fact is that Van Dyke was not a desert lover of the kind who excites today's desert rhapsodists. Quite to the contrary, he was an elitist Art for Art's Sake devotee, the associate of some of the richest people in the world, and the hail-fellow-well-met of such flamboyant artists as James McNeill Whistler and Julius L. Stewart. The writer's legerdemain, then, tells us much about Van Dyke but also much about our society.

In the closing decades of the last century, the country's recent industrialization provided a small fraction of financially privileged people the leisure to indulge their whims and enjoy the benefits of music, painting, and other aspects of culture.[2] Among this segment were many admirably generous, enlightened, and public-spirited figures who, enviably buoyed with nineteenth-century optimism, addressed the nation's problems. Other men preferred to look down on the middle and lower classes. Reacting to the very ugliness their smokestacks and workers' slums were creating, some of the new devotees of refinement sniffed at realism in art as a sign of low taste. To them, escape into beautiful illusion was what mattered, and hence to lead a double life or to write books of beautiful fantasies not only was expected, it was all but *de rigueur.* As Van Dyke himself summed up the general attitude, the purpose of art "is to give pleasure, not to inculcate truth" (*Principles of Art* 185–86). Yet as part of their elaborate games, such people sometimes maintained nearly impenetrable disguises, their private jokes on the literally minded unfortunates far down the ladder in the workaday world. In Van Dyke the fabulous urge exhibited itself in subtle detail as well as in the larger aspects of his life. On the first count, for instance, he dedicates *The Desert* (vii) not to some well-known nature lover and preservationist of the day such as John Muir but—coyly using initials only—to nature-wrecking steel mogul Andrew Carnegie (Ingham and Wild).

Another jewel of an example in this department is Van Dyke's letter (included below) in the Arizona Historical Society to Robert H. Forbes, a professor of agriculture at the University of Arizona. Nailed by the scientist for the mistakes riddling *The Desert*, Van Dyke pretends thanks and contrition. In a tangle of obfuscation, he first pleads that, well, mistakes occur in every book. He next blames the written sources he has consulted. Then, turning logic on its head, Van Dyke bemoans the *lack* of written sources. He next makes a wild suggestion: that he misquote another professor. This is a bizarre, squidlike performance. The supreme irony, however, is that Van Dyke, remaining aloof despite Forbes's knowledge, made only a gesture of mending the many twisted facts in his "corrected" edition of *The Desert.*

Such is Van Dyke's thumbing of his nose at the public that

came to adore *The Desert*—a public, in any case, he thought too dull to understand his book. In the larger picture, even Van Dyke's recently published *Autobiography* keeps up its author's pose as a rugged outdoorsman (117–22). In line with this and helping to preserve the ruse, most of Van Dyke's personal papers have disappeared, possibly Van Dyke's own doing.

Van Dyke's scattered letters, then, become extremely important. In them we catch the best glimpses of the "real" Van Dyke as he lets his public guard down. However, it should be added as an aside that there was something impish in the man, an indication that at times he also wanted to be followed, albeit not without first extracting considerable labor from future scholars. Bearing witness to this is the "McLuckie" letter (Theo. Sem., June 29, 1898),[3] an arresting revelation about Van Dyke's activities. Yet it is a letter not only preserved by Van Dyke in his own library but inscribed with instructions for its interpretation. In any case, in the following pieces we see the bagman for industrialist Andrew Carnegie, the shrewd buyer of art, the holier-than-thou aesthetician—in short, we catch Van Dyke's elusive qualities that influenced the shape of his finely drawn prose, that lie at the very heart of the best book ever written about the desert.

And so the ironies turn on themselves. *The Desert* hardly is a fraud in the common sense of the word; rather, it is the result of a finely spun aesthetic held by a coterie of art lovers on the East coast and romantically imposed upon a distant landscape. Because of this, the identification of Van Dyke's art associates and their paintings in the letters is particularly important. Art for Art's Sake and the related impressionism emphasized not only nature as the greatest art but also the use of color and light to capture fleeting moments. Van Dyke's *The Desert* is just such a work, using the imagery of prose to capture what Van Dyke's artist friends were doing with paint. In fact, perhaps in a wry reference to this relationship, Van Dyke uses the very word *impression* in the preface of his famous book (xi).[4] *The Desert*, then, is a book of beautiful illusions written by a man who often lived in a high-toned world of artistic illusions.[5]

Critics at least since Franklin Walker have said as much (186–87), repeating the comment about Van Dyke's transfer of artistic values to desert landscapes. Yet, though the observation certainly is true, it is inadequate, for it tells us only in the vaguest terms what kind of seeing Van Dyke brought to the desert. The tenets of Art for Art's Sake and impressionism are so hazy and various that to say Van Dyke was entranced by the forms and colors of the arid lands is to say very little on the score. When Van Dyke hails the desert as "the most decorative landscape in the world, a landscape all color, a dream landscape," his rhetoric is persuasively emotional but inexact. On the same page, he comes a bit closer to definition by lauding the sensuousness of the desert, based on its simple lines and finest colors (56). But upon examination, the statement makes little sense. The simplest form of landscape surely would be the flatness of the Great Plains, the steppes, or the unrelieved arctic stretches, not the serrated ranges and intermittent cactus sweeps of the Southwest. And what exactly does he mean by finest colors? As stated here, the preference seems more idiopathic than formulaic. On top of the vagueness, considering the inconsistencies and downright contradictions among Van Dyke's many statements about art, what values from that mass did he pick to apply to the Southwest?[6] This is a large issue, one concerning how we today, following Van Dyke's lead, see the deserts. Once again we seem lost in a welter of conflicting pronouncements by the mercurial writer.

And once again, Van Dyke's letters lead to an answer sharpening the formerly blurred understanding of the man and his work. Though a woozy indefiniteness reigns in such books as *What Is Art?*, in other works Van Dyke brings himself to task as a precise seer. His correspondence with the editors of the *Century Magazine*, in the holdings of the New York Public Library, reveal him in just such a precise mode when writing the series of articles later collected in the handsome volume *Old English Masters.* Discussing the features of specific paintings reproduced in the magazine and analyzing them for a middle-class audience, Van Dyke treats the effects of details, the loveliness of hair trailing off into the background and the brightness of a bodice reflecting light on a face. Then, too, he was cooperating on the project with Timothy Cole, the engraver who produced the illustrations for the series, and Van Dyke may have been influenced by the experience of working intimately, indeed happily, with demanding and perceptive Cole and by the precision of a craftsman who likely would brook no emptily aureate pronouncements from his coworker.

Here, the critic who elsewhere could heap coals upon the heads of realistic painters for playing to lowbrow audiences turns remarkably evenhanded, accepting artists on their own terms and praising them for their degree of success achieved while working toward the aesthetic goals set for themselves. Yet Van Dyke also is restrained in his encomiums, honoring the cows and clouds of landscapist John Constable, for example, but only so far, concluding somewhat backhandedly that "he is not undeserving of painters' praise" (197).

Only once in the entire series does Van Dyke abandon his guard and speak with an enthusiasm from the viscera, and it is for Joseph M. W. Turner, a painter slowly going mad and, ever more excited by the process, painting his own madness (173–87). With the passing years, Turner's canvases grow ever more wild, distorting scenes with blurs of pyrotechnic colors and writhing shapes. Yet it is this very abandon to extravagance—his very flights beyond reality—that appeals to the excited Van Dyke. Applauding the increasingly maddened man soaring above mundane facts, Van Dyke harrumphs that "he carried his nature in his imagination, and he painted his pictures out of his head. . . . His landscapes have no existence in nature" (181).

Here, with Turner, where Van Dyke is never more earnest, never more avidly empathetic with an artist, he is speaking of himself, of his own proud falseness and extravagances of color and writhing forms. It should be emphasized that Van Dyke was working on his Old English Masters series during the very period he was writing *The Desert.* His ebullient chapter on Turner, then, is a window into his artistic thinking at the time. When we view such an otherworldly painting as the famed Turner seascape *The Fighting Téméraire*, we are looking through a blazing lens of oils and through the prose of Van Dyke's *The Desert* to the real desert, now wondrously distorted (Wild, "How a London Madman Painted Our Deserts").

As will be seen, these were not always happy soarings. Perhaps more than most of us, the illusionist, the seeker of the ideal, inevitably fails and is pained by his failure to achieve his goal; and the person who rants against the stupidity of the masses may well do so, turning his ire outward, because he finds so much to despise when he looks into his own soul.

It should be emphasized that the following is only a sampling of letters and that they in turn reveal only a sampling, though, we think, a significant one, of Van Dyke as he lived his daily life and thought his daily thoughts. The letters are full of contradictions—to be expected from a man who throve on deception. Hence, the person who scorns his reading public next does a gleeful jig when his desert book sells well. The man who claims in his autobiography that while wandering in the desert he accidentally discovered gold but would not deign to take any, next hounds his editor over a mistake in a royalty payment of a mere $1.65. In such things, then, the letters need to be read with an eye toward subtlety, toward piecing together a man full of contradictions, a man who at times said the opposite of what he meant.

Some of the features here are fairly obvious, as is Van Dyke's rascally, biting humor. Others need some context. For instance, throughout his life Van Dyke was plagued by a variety of illnesses. These, as he says, turned him into a "crank," but one is left wondering which resulted from which, the illnesses from his bouts of depression or his funks from his physical maladies. One wonders, too, how much the accepted but wrongheaded remedies of the day exacerbated or perhaps caused his conditions, affecting his mood swings and thus influencing similar swings in his prose. This is dramatically suggested, as we will see, in the doses of silver nitrate Van Dyke was taking (Am. Academy, October 25, 1909). In any case, despite his debilitation and frequent absences for travel, both Rutgers and the Seminary thought Van Dyke such a prize on their campuses that they indulged him to the point of lavishness—to the extent that the Seminary built a house on its campus specifically for Van Dyke.

Not so obvious also are other implications lurking beneath the polished surfaces of some of the following letters. Hitherto unknown to Van Dyke scholars is the friendship between southwestern booster Charles F. Lummis and John C. Van Dyke.[7] Superficially, Van Dyke's congratulations to Lummis on his sixty-fourth birthday (Southwest Museum, February 12, 1923) would seem but a gentlemanly courtesy from one well-known writer to another.

But as it turns out, the "Spanish dinner" Van Dyke alludes to occurred fifteen years before, as recorded in Lummis's diary (Southwest Museum, July 30, 1908). Thus, given Van Dyke's frequent trips to southern California, the relationship between the two men may have been a long one.

Both men had their flamboyant streaks. Lummis, who beat his literary drum loudly for what he touted as the near-religious enchantment of the Southwest, strutted about in the costume of a Spanish grandee, complete with sombrero and sash, a bombastic (and in today's terms, embarrassing) one-man PR show. It is amusing to picture these two foxes cavorting through an evening of "wine, women, and song." More telling beyond that is Van Dyke's acceptance of a man déclassé in terms of the refined professor's personal reserve and public aesthetics. One can imagine that Van Dyke considered such an evening a delightful *opéra bouffe*, an amusing but harmless entertainment to be enjoyed on his visits to the cultural outback of Los Angeles. Furthermore, contrary to the nasty situation that developed between Van Dyke and sophisticated novelist Edith Wharton, Van Dyke could have felt little threat from Lummis, a man safely distant both geographically and intellectually.

A related but somewhat different anomaly obtains in the correspondence concerning Van Dyke and another Californian, writer and photographer J. Smeaton Chase (Prince. Univ., Scribner's Archives, April 20, 1915, September 17, 1917, September 18, 1917, and October 4, 1917). In 1918, encouraged both by the book's robust sales and by Van Dyke's hearty endorsement, Scribner's brought out an illustrated edition of *The Desert* featuring work by Chase. Ironically, the illustrations violated Van Dyke's own artistic tenets, for *The Desert* was a painting in prose, describing, in Van Dyke's words, "the desert from an esthetic . . . point of view" (*Autobiography* 240 n. 2). According to the stance, the realism of photographs was to be abhorred. Further, *The Desert* was a "pure" work of aestheticism, its focus on nature, not on human-interest aspects such as cowboys, Indians, eccentric sourdoughs and other such features then becoming popular with tourists. Yet transgressing his own principles, which despised the "human element" in art (168), the photographs Van Dyke approved baldly display a human figure, saddled horses, and a shotgun leaning against a cactus to show scale. To further insult the aesthetic reprobate, Van Dyke says he mixed in with Chase's work a sampling of his own pictures. Doing all this in fine fettle, the elitist aesthete turned entrepreneur and now clapped his hands at the ringing bells of the cash registers.

That was not the first of Van Dyke's tricks when it came to photographs. In reference to the frontispiece Van Dyke passes on to his editor for use in the original edition of *The Desert* (Prince. Univ., May 23, 1901), George Wharton James, a desert writer following close on Van Dyke's heels, alleges that Van Dyke stole the picture from him (*Wonders of the Colorado Desert* 1: xxix). In any case, adding to the atmosphere of connivery, Van Dyke's frontispiece is a dramatic vista of the Painted Desert, an area not discussed at length in the book's pages.[8]

Many of the letters crackle with double meanings, with private jokes and innuendoes whose intent is not always immediately clear. For instance, James Bertram, Carnegie's secretary, alludes to Van Dyke's involvement in a kidnapping threat (Theo. Sem., October 20, 1921). The aura of intrigue and delight in weaving conspiracies is quite in keeping with the life of a wily bachelor who, as part of his legacy, left not only a daughter, Clare, but a gold ring engraved with a coded inscription.[9] On such matters, since the letters hardly speak for themselves, their editors sift through the context of Van Dyke's life to suggest the underlying reality.

Van Dyke could be a person of many moods, unpredictably swinging to the poles of emotion. He can on the one hand address his editor in a demanding tone (Prince. Univ., May 23, 1901), then in the next letter beg the man for guidance (Prince. Univ., June 4, 1901). Van Dyke writes a graciously entertaining account of his travels in *The Open Spaces*, then turning self-righteous damns (and offends) just about everyone with the intemperate tirade of *The Money God.* At the age of seventy, the traveler writes his editor a rakish letter from the Canal Zone, including a bit of doggerel and winking that in Panama "everything forbidden" is available (Prince. Univ., January 7, 1926). He snaps at the person offering him a national honor (Am. Academy, March 3, 1908), then becomes sugary in accepting another honor from the same person

(Am. Academy, December 6, 1923). He writes a heartfelt letter of condolence to a dear friend (Colum. Univ., February 5, 1924).

Whatever the swings, Van Dyke also knew how to mind his manners when necessary. He consistently cloaked himself in polite deference when treating with Andrew Carnegie, a man who could make, or break, huge chunks of Van Dyke's career. If there is any doubt about Van Dyke's contempt for the hoi polloi, his personal communications should dispel it. In sending the manuscript of *The Desert* to Scribner's, Van Dyke sniffs at the "swash" of popular writing and implies that what he writes is so good that the common herd will not be able to fathom it (Prince. Univ., May 23, 1901). Twenty years later, he rants about noisome inquiries from the public and informs his secretary that he consigns such irritations to the wastebasket (Am. Academy, December 19, 1923).

It is true that we know from people who remember Van Dyke that he could be personally aloof, if not unapproachable. Yet our judgment should be tempered somewhat, for his associates, the culture-bearers of the time, were trying to combat what they saw as the vulgarity of prevailing tastes. These indeed ran to illustrations of maidens crying their hearts out under weeping willow trees. One of the authorities of the day felt no compunction about lecturing against the blockheadedness of a "general public," which should look to its educated betters, "the critics," if it ever hoped to be elevated above bathos (Van Rensselaer). As it happens, the writer was Mariana Griswold (Mrs. Schuyler) Van Rensselaer, Van Dyke's early mentor. In this, Van Dyke followed Mrs. Van Rensselaer's lead. Speaking ex cathedra, he made no bones about attacking sentimentality in art. He scorned "anything that is of popular interest" (*What Is Art?* 87), words that a middle class eager to "be cultured" avidly read, though reluctantly followed.

A hundred years later, in an age far more democratized, prosperous, and educated, it is easy to forget the gilt-edged exclusivity of Van Dyke's circles. We find Van Dyke, born in a mansion, summering in his spacious house in the Catskills—this at the Onteora Club, one of the most fashionable developments for the wealthy of the day, one with a guard at the gate to keep out the riffraff (Am. Academy, September 12, 1926).[10] When Van Dyke holds discussions with J. Smeaton Chase about illustrating *The Desert*, the professor meets him in the hushed paneled halls of the Century Club—something that must have left the impecunious photographer from the West, arriving in New York City with his hat in his hand and hoping for the $100 payment that would turn his fortunes, dazzled (Prince. Univ., October 4, 1917). When Van Dyke writes up a list of intimates to receive engraved invitations for attendance at the functions of the tony American Academy of Arts and Letters, the roster includes a countess and the wife of the richest man in America (undated; appears after Am. Academy, October 25, 1909).

A word or two is in order on the Academy, which held itself in high esteem. It consisted of two intertwined groups, the 250 artists, writers, musicians, and such of the National Institute of Arts and Letters, and 50 members chosen from that body to be elevated into the American Academy of Arts and Letters. In referring to both bodies as one entity, the following uses simply "the Academy." Elected to the National Institute in 1908, Van Dyke served as its president from 1924 to 1925. The Academy of Arts and Letters gave Van Dyke the nod in 1923. Yet not all was placid in the bosom of the august institution.[11] Since its officers were scattered about the country, Van Dyke, himself a frequent traveler, chafed, trying to conduct business by letter from afar and despairing that he could assemble a quorum of committee members in one place to conduct business. Consequently, he depended on Mrs. Vanamee,[12] the secretarial assistant to the president, to keep the machinery running, feed him information on developing intrigues, and soothe bruised egos.

There is an irony in Mrs. Vanamee's crucial role among these self-important personages. In Van Dyke's day, the Academy, basically a "boys' club" of often feuding old men with conservative, if not rigid, dispositions, fought to keep out changes as if they were tradition-wrecking invaders pounding at the door. Van Dyke was among the hand-wringers inside. However, he could bend. Van Dyke scowls at Carl Sandburg, a "tramp poet" in the professor's estimation, but Van Dyke, proud of his family connections to Lincoln (*Autobiography* 11–16), allows that maybe the celebrant of slaughterhouses might be let in because of his two volumes on the former president (Am. Academy, September 12, 1926). Van Dyke was not so generous when it came to women. In a letter not reproduced, he wails to Mrs. Vanamee about "that woman question" (Am. Academy, November 9, 1925). Though eventually he relented, Van Dyke for years threw his lot with those who opposed the nomination of women to the Academy, particularly the nomination of novelist Edith Wharton (Am. Academy, November 5, 1925; November 9, 1925; not reproduced, August 29, 1932).[13] Though his was not a fashionable act in today's terms, a rush to condemn Van Dyke by applying current wisdom to a different age struggling with its own dynamics would be wrong. As Van Dyke's deference to the instruction of Mrs. Van Rensselaer bears out, he was no more a misogynist than the women of the day were misandrists. Rather, to Van Dyke's late-Victorian mind, order in formal social matters was the essence of good sense, and he probably thought that if the Academy wanted to be a "boys' club," it had that right.

Furthermore, good breeding is not a sure alexipharmic to the testy edges of human nature, and a more intimate ire may have been at work here. Despite their cultured upbringings, both Van Dyke and Edith Wharton had rather nappy personalities, and the fact that at Scribner's they shared the same editor, William C. Brownell, likely increased the rivalry between these two ego-driven writers (Bell 53–54).[14] For her part, Wharton had poured her measure of gasoline onto the fire. Appearing in Wharton's novel *The House of Mirth* is art connoisseur Ned Van Alstyne, a womanizing reactionary with a sarcastic tongue sounding very much like Van Dyke.[15] However, far more came into play here than the clawing and scratching of two well-known writers. Part of the Old Guard threatened by the swordpoints of change, Van Dyke could not have been pleased by Mrs. Wharton's satirical novels about high society, and this has nothing to do with either her sex or her sharp edges. A writer might have a good guffaw playing jokes on the public, depicting himself romping off on wild buffalo hunts or just for the fun of it hoodwinking readers with fetching stories about the dwarf deer encountered in the far-off deserts. However, to tell tales out of school, as Edith Wharton did volubly in her novels, was a betrayal of one's class, a dangerous violation not readily forgiven.[16]

That is, it was not that wealthy late Victorians did not have their fun; they just did not feel compelled, as do celebrities in our present day, to flaunt the details of their sometimes sizzling lives before the public. For the sake of "ordinary discretion," Van Dyke keeps a gentleman's silence and demurs when it comes to his love affairs (*Autobiography* 132). Thus we get the tension within a writer who on the one hand projected a make-believe image as stalwart romantic hero to his reading public but on the other kept his private but lively affairs secret. For instance, with a little ferreting we find him sailing the seas with a shipload of beauties on the most sumptuous private yacht of the day. The floating palace, complete with spiral staircase and elegant stained glass by Tiffany, was owned by the notorious playboy and daredevil millionaire James Gordon Bennett Jr.[17]

Not so easily ferreted out is the matter of Van Dyke's child, Clare Van Dyke Parr, and though as a private issue it would not be of concern to us here, the letters supply added though veiled evidence supporting the possibility that she had much to do with Van Dyke's trip to the Southwest resulting in *The Desert.* In its pages, Van Dyke leads us to believe that he traveled through the region as a self-appointed "lover" of the desert's beauty (xi). In contrast, the *Autobiography* states health reasons for the trip (118, 122), reasons validated by what we know of Van Dyke's chronic respiratory condition. Yet, consciously or not, Van Dyke also drops hints that serious personal problems in New Brunswick propelled him from the East to his brother's ranch in the Mojave Desert of southern California.

A world traveler of wide experience and a methodical person who planned his life well in advance, Van Dyke usually was not a rash man when he began his journeys. But when he leaves for the desert, he does so all at once, precipitously resigning from his clubs and two academic positions and hitting the road on the run (116).[18] Once he gets to the desert, he finds it a place he does not particularly like (125), and he wanders about aimless and depressed, wanting to return to his home but unable to because there "seemed no alternative" (122). In other words, he sounds very much like a man on the lam. Now as it happened, Clare's mother, it is said, was the wife of one of Van Dyke's fellow faculty members (Strong x–xi). There are indications that about this time a fuss flared up about Clare and her relationship to Van Dyke (Wild, "Interviews and Notes"). Whether involving Clare or some other private aspect of his life, the problem stung Van Dyke, and it was not resolved even after his desert travels. While roaming the West, he must have kept the pulse of things back in New Brunswick. Writing from Texas before departing the Southwest for home, he makes reference to an unfavorable climate awaiting him and fears that he may have to "emigrate again" (Prince. Univ., May 23, 1901). Then, after his return to New Jersey, he tells his editor at Scribner's that the heat is "infernal" and that he wants to "get out fast" (Prince. Univ., June 2 [1902 or 1903])—hardly a comment on meteorological conditions. At the time, there was no heat wave in New Brunswick. Quite to the contrary: though doubt surrounds the year of this letter, during the week Van Dyke wrote it, either in 1902 or in 1903, the temperature was about normal.[19] Even if the weather had been oppressive, Wilkes-Barre, Pennsylvania, Van Dyke's destination about a hundred miles inland from New Brunswick, hardly would have been the place to escape it. Yet as will be seen, possible trouble over Clare was not the sole impetus for Van Dyke's flight to the Southwest.

Meanwhile, Van Dyke's mention to his editor of matters having little or nothing to do with ongoing literary projects may strike us as strange, but it brings up the issue of yet another special person in Van Dyke's life. In a far different way than did Clare, William C. Brownell had much to do with the shape of *The Desert* we read today.

Van Dyke probably acknowledges his aesthetic debt to Mrs. Van Rensselaer because at the time of her help he was a youth in need of guidance. He respected the ministrations of an older and cultured woman from his own class and Dutch subculture. After that, Van Dyke's swelling ego took over. After that, once launched in the direction of Art for Art's Sake, he charged about, acidly ridiculing the opinions of other authorities and haughtily measuring himself only by his own often contradictory standards. That was Van Dyke's crusty public exterior. However, if half his heart was adamantine and steely cold, the other half—

the one he rarely disclosed—was warm, pink, and fuzzy. The private Van Dyke was a rank sentimentalist, as shown by this scene remembered from the mansion of his childhood:

> Among my earliest memories was that of the long music room at Green Oaks, with my mother seated at a blue-and-red-piped organ singing "Long, Long Ago." I can see myself seated on the floor playing with toys, the room darkened to keep out the heat, and my mother dressed in white. There was a large glass chandelier hanging from the ceiling, and a stray sunbeam striking the prisms threw a halo of color about her head. I have always remembered that picture and the sadness of "Long, Long Ago" and "Gaily the Troubadour," which she sang out of a large music book. (*Autobiography* 26)

Tortured between the poles of emotions, Van Dyke, to his credit, recognized his weakness for saccharine writing, but in this he could not control his pen. Fortunately, he found a confidant in his editor at Scribner's. Thus in discussing the manuscript of *The Desert*, Van Dyke unabashedly throws himself at the feet of William C. Brownell, begging the editor to save him from his own "idiocies" and desperately hoping that Brownell will keep him from "making too big an ass of myself" (Prince. Univ., June 4 [1901]). Such pleas occur throughout Van Dyke's correspondence with Brownell.

This was an astounding act of self-humiliation and personal revelation for a man of Van Dyke's pride. It also was an immensely beneficial one. In books written without Brownell's guidance, such as *The Story of the Pine*—a story about a love affair between two trees—we see how badly Van Dyke could plunge off the tracks into sentimental swamps. Van Dyke felt comfortable with Brownell; the courtly editor was of Van Dyke's class—wealthy, erudite, and refined—and he was gently understanding but firm. We do not know the exact details of Brownell's guidance, but we do know that, while he sympathized with Van Dyke's aesthetics, the kind and emotionally stable Brownell was a thorough copy editor and that he held excessive emotion up to realistic scrutiny (Lewis 132–33, Bates 172–74). He likely reined in Van Dyke from his more romantic flights, and to Brownell may well go the credit for the hard, clear edges of *The Desert*'s memorable imagery.

The letters reveal yet a third person who profoundly influenced the making of the desert's most famous book, though in this, as with Clare, mystery continues to shroud the issue. We have already commented on Van Dyke's submissive tone when dealing with Andrew Carnegie, and well did Van Dyke tread lightly around this eminent American who cast a shadow of omnipotence. Certainly Van Dyke's ego was involved in the relationship. About thirty miles southwest of New York City, New Brunswick was out in the sticks, at least in the minds of people at the crowded center of America's culture. Cows still mooed within earshot of Van Dyke's two campuses, and the professor worried that sophisticated urbanites would notice the dirt on his shoes. In a letter not reproduced, he tries to make a joke of his embarrassment: "I am simply an unfortunate wretch living in the country" (Colum. Univ., January 14, 1915).

Given this, the overwhelmingly powerful Carnegie lent Van Dyke cachet. It is not clear if because of the relationship Carnegie, who distributed his largesse by the millions to educational institutions, donated either to Rutgers or to the Theological Seminary. We do know, however, that Van Dyke was the most successful fund raiser the Seminary ever had. He solicited art work from his friends and raised the money to install intricate stained-glass windows, turning his Sage Library into the light-filled legacy of grace it is today. He furthermore whipped up financial support to build an extensive addition to complete the library's original Romanesque plan (Wild, "Interviews and Notes"). No doubt, it was a feather in Van Dyke's academic cap to take a man of Carnegie's stature strolling across the two campuses (Lib. of Congress, May 18, 1893). Because of his association with Carnegie, Van Dyke also had clout with artists, then, as now, usually threadbare in their finances. In Van Dyke's autobiography we see the industrialist dashing off checks for $1,000, then $5,000—huge amounts for the day—and finally giving Van Dyke "carte blanche" to buy any painting he wanted for Carnegie's growing collection of canvases (77). As the following Smithsonian correspondence dramatically illustrates, because of Carnegie's prestige and money, Van Dyke was a highly blessed man.

Yet if Carnegie took the younger man under his wing, inviting him to fishing expeditions at his castle in Scotland, to be followed by tea with the ladies on the moors, there was a darker side to the relationship, for America's most successful Captain of Industry, whatever his heralded magnanimity, amassed his fortune by trampling on his competitors and opponents. The bizarre "McLuckie" letter reproduced below offers evidence that Carnegie used Van Dyke for far more than a consultant for the industrialist's dallyings in art and, as an added benefit, a witty contributor to the polite repartee around Carnegie's tea table (Theo. Scm., Junc 29, 1898).

Behind literature can lie strange provenances. This takes us back to the bloodiest labor strike in American history. In 1892, Carnegie unleashed three hundred Pinkerton guards on strikers at the Carnegie steel mill in Homestead, Pennsylvania. After the smoke cleared from the ensuing shootout, nearly twenty men lay dead and many more were wounded. Carnegie had shrewdly directed events from overseas, sending his battle plans by international telegraph. However, though he got back his steel mill, he did so at great cost to his reputation, for the mud of his scheming stuck to him. Some newspapers exposed the steel magnate's brutality and betrayal of his workers. That grated on philanthropist Carnegie, who liked to keep a clean image with the public. As a result of the continuing bad publicity, he had his agents hound John McLuckie, one of the strike leaders, until he fled for his life into Mexico.[20]

However, Carnegie's *Autobiography* gave the industrialist the opportunity to retell the story and cast this blemish on his record in a happy light. He does so by including an account written for the purpose by Van Dyke, who also happened to have edited the autobiography after Carnegie's death—thus making the record doubly suspect. In any case, Van Dyke recites a wonderful coincidence. In 1900, while traveling in Mexico as part of his trip to the Southwest, he chanced to meet none other than the poverty-stricken McLuckie. According to this version of the story, Van Dyke contacted Carnegie, whose heart now softened at the plight of the bedraggled former striker. Carnegie directed Van Dyke to rescue McLuckie with an anonymous gift of money. Though McLuckie refused the offer, Van Dyke managed to pull some strings and get him a job on the American-run railroad in northern Mexico. When Van Dyke later told McLuckie who had offered the money, the former striker was "stunned" and his heart overflowed with goodwill toward Carnegie (235–39).

As might be guessed, the account reeks of a public-relations job that pretties up the truth for public consumption. Though research has not revealed all the facts of the McLuckie issue, the Carnegie letter printed below does far more than cast a dubious light on the version in Carnegie's autobiography. Here, the joshing of Van Dyke for joining the "capitalistic class," the delight at Van Dyke's "success," even the jocular misspelling of Van Dyke's address—together, of course, with Carnegie's handwritten instructions to Van Dyke and Carnegie's additional command to Van Dyke to erase the implicating note—signal a quite different reality behind the McLuckie story, as does the date, two years earlier than the account in Carnegie's *Autobiography*. This indicates not the chance meeting of Van Dyke's public version but a long-term involvement with McLuckie. Such circumstances point to Van Dyke's acting as a bagman for Carnegie to pay off McLuckie and keep him safely in Mexico.

They point, too, to Van Dyke's penchant, not only for inflating some of his deeds into romantic fictions, but also for playing his cards close to the vest when it came to some other details of his personal life. One might puzzle, for instance, that Van Dyke dates his preface for *The Desert* from La Noria Verde, a place he obliquely refers to several times elsewhere in his writings. One might puzzle even more upon finding the place. As it turns out, La Noria Verde is in Mexico, and it appears on the topographic maps as a few scattered buildings out on the desert flats north of Hermosillo, Sonora.[21] What on earth would the august art critic and habitué of salons hung with impressionist paintings be doing in such a frayed-at-the-cuffs place, one not likely different from the many humble ranchitos scattered across dusty Sonora?

We still don't have the complete story, but a visit to the "ranchito" certainly points toward an answer, one—as with so many other things about Van Dyke—at once surprising and, in retrospect at least, expected. There in the middle of the desert one sees, not the imagined adobe shanties with chickens running in the yard, but the arched and colonnaded ruins of an enormous hacienda. This is the abandoned estate of the rich and politically powerful Aguilar family, complete, for those disposed to scenes appropriate to Gothic novels, with its own ruined chapel and two ancient women, the descendants of servants from better days, still living mysteriously in the nearby rubble.

So once again Van Dyke, an elegant fox, has shown himself true to form.

Along such lines, much surrounding the writing of *The Desert* cannot be proven. Yet it seems clear that much besides nature appreciation lay behind the writing of the desert's most famous book. We do not know if Van Dyke traveled to the Southwest as a nature lover, for his health, because of an uproar over Clare, or as an agent for Carnegie. Possibly, all of these factors came into play. Given the complexity and secrecy of the refined aesthetician's life, such would fit the pattern. One thing we do have to credit Van Dyke with. When he passed through the Southwest, he did what he often did when he traveled: he transcended his troubles and wrote a book praising the beauty of what he saw around him, and that marked the inception of our present views of the region.

Some word should be said about the places in Van Dyke's life. After all, he was a peripatetic aesthete who roamed the world searching for visual feasts, whether in nature or in the museums of Vienna or St. Petersburg. Then, too, when he was still a fairly young man he lost both his parents, and his brothers scattered, leaving him to make a lifetime roost in New Brunswick, the old hometown where, except for himself, the Van Dyke dynasty, with its mansion out in the countryside, now occupied by strangers, was but a memory. In this sense psychically homeless, Van Dyke the bachelor was the new modern man, attaching himself to a series of places with varying degrees of impermanence. For the most part, they were other people's places, and one suspects he held them dear as does the itinerant outsider, for a brief time enjoying someone else's stable homelife.

On the one extreme were places like Onteora, the salons and clubs of New York City, London, and Venice, and Carnegie's opulent, if rather monstrous, castle in Scotland—either sophisticated urban places or outposts where urbanites transferred their wealth and sophistication into the country.

Yet true to Van Dyke's dualistic nature, he also swung to the other pole. And there we find him on a rawboned little ranch on the Mojave Desert near the crude little boomtown of Daggett, California, a town so crude and sporadically wild with silver miners celebrating their strikes that the locals took pride in the town's evil reputation. They even took pride in the fact that when a shootout left a man dead on the floor of the crowded Bucket of Blood Saloon, no witnesses could be found.[22]

Yet Van Dyke's presence in Daggett doubtless had more to do with his health and his admiration for elder brother Theodore than with a latent fascination for the Wild West in the breast of the New Jersey aesthete. In the 1870s, while searching for an agreeable climate, brother Theodore had settled in southern California, and over the decades brother John, also afflicted with respiratory problems, paid periodic visits. A graduate of Princeton, Theodore was an attorney, an able outdoorsman—as his brother was not—and a novelist. Despite its isolation, his ranch became a crossroads for naturalists, who were just then beginning to "discover" the desert as a fascinating place. Theodore also was Daggett's no-nonsense justice of the peace, a respected position in an area where men were wild and the law was thin, one earning him the title of Judge.

Fortunately for us, Theodore's son Dix wrote his reminiscences of life in Daggett, portions of which appear below. Exactly what the trouble was between renowned explorer and conservationist John Muir and John C. Van Dyke we may never know, though given Dix's backhanded tone in describing his uncle, one suspects pretentiousness may have been at its root. Fortunately, too, isolated Daggett remains much as it was when John C. Van Dyke visited—a gift remaining from the nineteenth-century frontier—with several of the ranch houses still standing and before one of them the very jail that Theodore kept at his ranch.[23]

Yet if the two poles of Van Dyke's life were fashionable salons on one end, brazen Daggett on the other, surely New Brunswick was its center. Here Van Dyke, sometimes frenetic in his avid comings and goings, found quiet balm in his campus home overlooking the Raritan River, in the steeples of the quaint college town, and in the woods beyond (*Autobiography* 208). Van Dyke did not try to disguise his love of the place. Out wandering the marshes in a snowstorm, he looks back on his beloved town perched on its hill:

> Far away across the marshes the air is blue-white, and through the veil of it one sees the arches of the great railroad bridge merely as a ghostly pattern. Tower and chimney, dome and steeple of the old town loom through the snow-mist, their higher pinnacles lost in the upper air. The dark river where the flakes are falling and disappearing runs across the foreground. What a black-and-white, with a cold tinge of blue and purple! (*The Meadows* 243–44)

Here, in his childhood hometown, Van Dyke found a balance to his busyness.

To end on a lighter note, we conclude with the last letter extant written to Van Dyke. No neoteric, for all his wiles Van Dyke despised what we would today call the glitz of modern society. In *The Meadows* Van Dyke rends his garments over a world gone mad with racing automobiles, wayward youth, and movies: "The rushing world craves the novel and exotic, and in seeking to avoid the obvious it only too often falls into admiration of the merely bizarre" (125). One can only wonder if Van Dyke, who had played his share of tricks on the public, shook his head sadly or chuckled over the successes of his nephew, famed movie director Woody Van Dyke, whose extravaganzas, such as *Tarzan the Ape Man*, were playing before an easily hoodwinked public.

For reading ease, the letters are arranged chronologically within the collections from which they are taken. This preserves consistency of theme and preserves the narratives played out in the various correspondences. The items in the Princeton University archives, for example, all deal with Van Dyke's relationship with Charles Scribner's Sons, Van Dyke's main publisher.

Concerning the format of the letters, all are handwritten unless otherwise identified. All the signatures also are handwritten unless otherwise noted. In order to preserve the flavor of individual writers, some peculiarities in their styles have been passed along intact. Generally, however, the spelling, punctuation, and other purely mechanical aspects of the texts have been regularized for ease of reading. Occasionally, the editors supply information in brackets. More extensive comments, as in the identification of people and works of art, appear in the notes. However, the intent is not to clutter the reading with notes but to concentrate on those features most helpful in understanding Van Dyke. In some cases throughout the correspondence, third persons have penciled in dates where they are lacking. These can be badly inaccurate, and the editors have supplied more reasonable dates, again in brackets, based on the content and context of the letters.

The centering of the writer's address indicates use of letterhead; otherwise, the writer's address appears to the right, above the date of the letter.

## NOTES

1. Students of desert history are fortunate to have W. Storrs Lee's *The Great California Deserts*, which shows how, beginning decades before Van Dyke's book, these and other factors evolved into today's favorable attitudes toward our arid lands. Franklin Walker's *A Literary History of Southern California* concentrates on the literary aspect of the shift. More generally, in *Wilderness and the American Mind* Roderick Nash traces the large shift over the course of American history from fear to appreciation of wild nature.

2. Two worthy explorations of the phenomenon and its consequences are Ronald G. Pisano's *Idle Hours: Americans at Leisure, 1865–1914* and Mary Cable's *Top Drawer: American High Society from the Gilded Age to the Roaring Twenties.*

3. In the following discussion of the major issues revealed by the correspondence, individual letters are identified in parentheses containing the abbreviated name of the collection, then the date of the letter.

4. For a discussion of Van Dyke's art theories, see Teague, "A Sometime Ruskinite in the Wilderness," and Wild, *John C. Van Dyke: The Desert* (25–35). Of further help in understanding Van Dyke's artistic tastes is his private art collection, in the holdings of the Zimmerli Voorhees Museum on the New Brunswick campus of Rutgers University.

5. As might be gathered from this, Art for Art's Sake was pretty much what individual devotees wanted it to be, and efforts to define the movement tend to fade into its gauzy qualities. Here is Guérard's stab: "As a Faith, Art for Art's Sake is a form of mysticism. It implies that Art is a direct revelation. The poet . . . acknowledges no authority but his own inspiration. His art is a law unto itself, for it transcends the laws of common morality and common sense" (xiii). Several hundred pages later, the enthusiastic critic is still stabbing: "Art for Art's Sake . . . is the thrill of wonder, the gaze from a peak in Darien, the road to Xanadu" (338).

6. Van Dyke's inconsistencies in his pronouncements about art can be overemphasized. Whatever his artistic drifts and enthusiasms of the moment, Van Dyke generally held firm on two counts: his appreciation of classical art, as represented by Rembrandt, and the thrall in which im-

pressionism held him. Given his traditional background, the first is expected. The second, though seemingly an outlier for a man of his stuffy background, also is consistent. It has much to do with his class and the doctrine of the elect of his Calvinism. Both bolstered his attitude that he was among the chosen. Impressionism was becoming the darling of some segments of the group Van Dyke held in esteem, the upper class, yet in his youth, at least, the taste was still fresh, not so widely accepted as to be common. Thus, he could be both rebel by embracing impressionism and traditionally allied. He also could feel one of the chosen, a thinker ahead of his time privileged to lead the unenlightened. This has more to it than the usual echoes of an aristocratic Calvinist convinced he has cornered the market on the truth. The Reformed Church in America, which ran the Seminary, had ministers ordained into the teaching order. Members were not merely humdrum classroom instructors of Greek and biblical history.

They also served as the consciences of the larger community, bringing up issues needing rectification in the church body. Though Van Dyke was not ordained, at the Seminary he dealt daily with those who were, and their authority and purpose rubbed off on him. For Van Dyke, art was a secularized religion. As he says in his autobiography, "It seems that most of my endeavors have been of a missionary kind—a telling people something, an advising and admonishing, a guiding and a girding. All my books of whatever name or nature are infused with this spirit, the missionary spirit of carrying the gospel of art and nature to the heathen" (128).

7. The link between the two men may have come about through Van Dyke's elder brother Theodore Strong Van Dyke. A longtime resident of southern California, nature writer Theodore was a frequent contributor to Lummis's magazine *Land of Sunshine.*

8. James's account of the photograph works out to a view near Leupp, in northern Arizona, looking south from Newberry Mesa toward the Little Colorado River.

9. Parr. Section 6 (a) describes the ring: "a gold band ring with the inscription 'Spiro Asti Si.'"

10. For a history of the Onteora Club and a sense of its lavishness, see Gaillard. The reference to the guard at the gate appears in the caption on page 8. With aggressive humility, the stately houses dotting the wooded hills of these grand estates were referred to as "cottages" and, furthermore, were named. Van Dyke's was known both as Upenuf and Laghet. For pictures of the house, see pages 17, 22; location map pages 20–21.

11. For an overview of the Academy, its organization, triumphs, and troubles, see Hellman.

12. Pronounced Va-nā′-mee.

13. In 1926, Edith Wharton was admitted. At the time, the Academy had had one woman member, since deceased—the venerable Julia Ward Howe, an eminently "safe" choice, as Edith Wharton was not (Lewis 460).

14. Further evidence on the score is Wharton's close friend and mentor Henry James, who also had Brownell as his editor (Bell 88). Crusty Van Dyke did not like James, either (Van Dyke, *Autobiography* 131). For more on prickly Wharton and the patient Brownell—a relationship paralleling his with Van Dyke—see Aronson.

15. Compare Wharton's portrait of Van Alstyne in *The House of Mirth* (215, 217–18, 223, 254–60, 355–58) with the Van Dyke emerging throughout

Wild, "Interviews and Notes Regarding John C. Van Dyke." It appears that Wharton had a sure grasp not only of Van Dyke's character but of the rumors circulating about him.

16. A distinction needs to be made here. Wharton was not attacking elegance but the vulgarity that had crept into a once-elegant society. In this sense, Wharton also was a reactionary and in many ways agreed with Van Dyke. The difference lay in their responses. In his typical doggedness, Van Dyke rose to defend what was rapidly becoming the flaking shell of social graces, while Wharton exposed its present desiccated condition.

17. Van Dyke, *Autobiography* 150, 243–44 n. 2. A photograph of the painting referred to in the note appears after 127.

Personal grace did not always accompany physical elegance. A shocked *haut monde* ostracized James Gordon Bennett Jr. when he arrived drunk at his girlfriend's New Year's Eve party and proceeded to urinate into her piano. In the aftermath of the scandal, feisty Bennett and the outraged brother of the insulted young lady fought what is said to have been the last duel in United States history (Cable 7–10).

A more typical example of Victorian accommodation in Van Dyke's circle of stately public manners is his secretary, Mrs. Vanamee. Rumor suggests that Mrs. Vanamee, a widow, lived with the male assistant librarian of the American Academy. Said an actress of the day of such matters: "You can do anything you like as long as you don't do it in the streets and frighten the horses" (Cable 198).

18. Van Dyke adds on this page that neither Rutgers nor the Seminary accepted his resignations. In a measure of the two institutions' esteem for Van Dyke, they held the appointments open for him until his return. Van Dyke was gone for more than two years.

19. *Weekly Home News* (New Brunswick, N.J.), June 5, 1902, 3 (weather for week past), and first page of issues May 26 through June 2, 1903.

20. For contrasting versions of Carnegie's role in the Homestead Strike, see Demarest (314) and Hacker (373–84).

21. *San Miguel de Horcacitas;* Almada.

22. For depictions of Daggett's gnarly waywardness, see Dix Van Dyke's reminiscences mentioned below, as well as his "Law on the Desert" and "Old Times in Daggett." With his sardonic journalist's eye, Harry Carr creates especially lurid, and very readable, vignettes of the Mojave's wild desert boomtowns, ruled by thugs and featuring fallen ladies offering their services in tents. His front-page "Wolves on the Desert," devoted to Daggett's evils, had Angelenos at once gasping and intrigued by the goings-on over the mountains, out in what city folks in the properly middle-class coastal cities referred to as the "cow counties."

23. For the context of Theodore's ranch beyond Dix's reminiscences of Daggett, see John C. Van Dyke's *Autobiography* (167–68); Wild, "A Writer in a Wild Frontier Town," along with *Theodore Strong Van Dyke;* and Wolfe. Outdoorsman Theodore likely was the source for much of the information in *The Desert*, thus compensating for John C. Van Dyke's limited desert experience (John C. Van Dyke, *Autobiography* xxix–xxx).

As a curious side note, stalwart conservationist John Muir had intimate, but not always happy, connections with the Van Dykes and the ranch (Wild, "John Muir and the Desert Connection"; "John Muir and the Van Dyke Ranch," parts 1 and 2).

*The reading room of the Gardner A. Sage Library of the New Brunswick Theological Seminary as it appeared during the tenure of John C. Van Dyke as director. Van Dyke himself is seated at his desk, center.*

*A select party at Andrew Carnegie's Cluny Castle in Scotland in 1894. From left to right, Mrs. Burton Harrison, John C. Van Dyke, Andrew Carnegie, Mrs. John Morley (standing), and John Morley, Secretary for Ireland (face blurred in original).*

*John C. Van Dyke's brother Theodore entertained illustrious guests at his ranch near Daggett, California. From right to left are John Muir, Theodore's son Dix Van Dyke, and Theodore Strong Van Dyke. The two women are most likely Muir's daughters Helen and Wanda.*

*John C. Van Dyke observing the locals in Biskrah, Algeria.*

*Van Dyke dated the preface for* The Desert *from La Noria Verde but gave no idea where or what that was. True to the author's opulent style, La Noria Verde has recently been discovered to be, not some humble Mexican rancho, but a great hacienda, now in ruins, of the Aguilar family of Sonora, Mexico. Courtesy of Leonardo Varela Espinosa.*

*John C. Van Dyke, pointing, with Edward Everett Ayer at the Grand Canyon.*

*Arizona's Painted Desert, the frontispiece photograph for the original edition of John C. Van Dyke's* The Desert *in 1901. Attribution of the photograph is disputed.*

*World traveler Van Dyke, center, at Ephesus, seated near Captain Smiley, with whom he traveled eventfully in Europe and Asia Minor in 1905.*

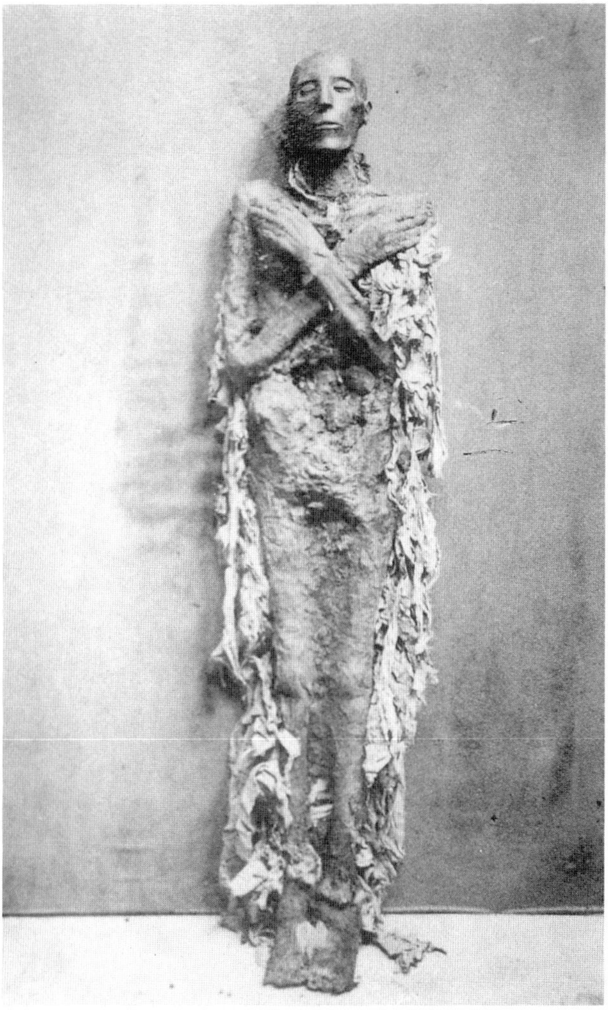

*Mummy of Seti I, Egyptian pharaoh of the Nineteenth Dynasty. Van Dyke was a mummy enthusiast, and his scrapbook in the Sage Library concludes with several mummy photographs, which he apparently collected during his travels in Egypt.*

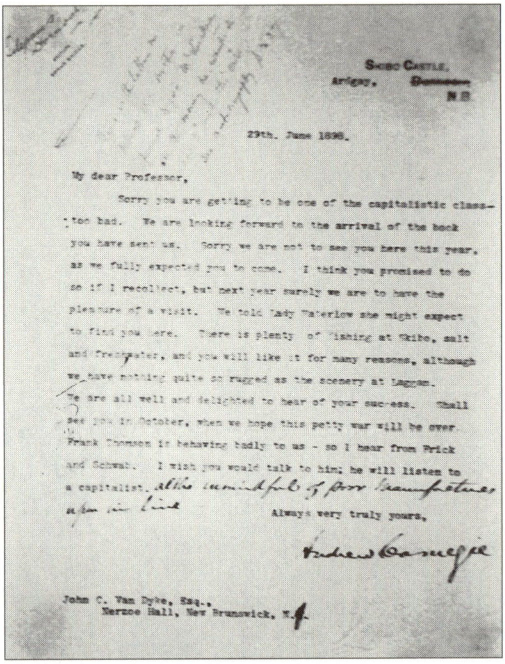

Skibo Castle,
Ardgay, N.B.

29th. June 1898.

My dear Professor,

Sorry you are getting to be one of the capitalistic class-too bad. We are looking forward to the arrival of the book you have sent us. Sorry we are not to see you here this year, as we fully expected you to come. I think you promised to do so if I recollect, but next year surely we are to have the pleasure of a visit. We told Lady Waterlow she might expect to find you here. There is plenty of fishing at Skibo, salt and freshwater, and you will like it for many reasons, although we have nothing quite so rugged as the scenery at Laggan. We are all well and delighted to hear of your success. Shall see you in October, when we hope this petty war will be over. Frank Thomson is behaving badly to us - so I hear from Frick and Schwab. I wish you would talk to him; he will listen to a capitalist. [illegible]

Always very truly yours,

John C. Van Dyke, Esq.,
Hertzog Hall, New Brunswick, N.J.

(above) Letter from Andrew Carnegie to Van Dyke from Skibo Castle, Scotland. (below) Letter from Booker T. Washington to Van Dyke, soliciting a one-dollar donation as part of a fund-raising effort for the Tuskegee Institute.

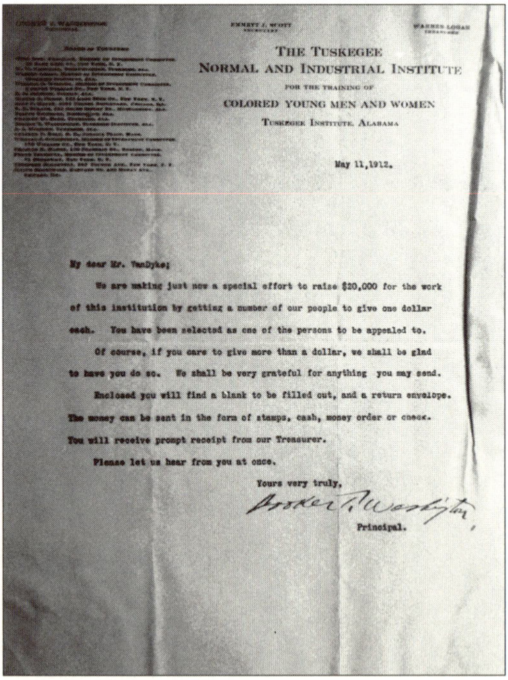

THE TUSKEGEE
NORMAL AND INDUSTRIAL INSTITUTE
FOR THE TRAINING OF
COLORED YOUNG MEN AND WOMEN
TUSKEGEE INSTITUTE, ALABAMA

May 11,1912.

My dear Mr. VanDyke;

We are making just now a special effort to raise $20,000 for the work of this institution by getting a number of our people to give one dollar each. You have been selected as one of the persons to be appealed to.

Of course, if you care to give more than a dollar, we shall be glad to have you do so. We shall be very grateful for anything you may send.

Enclosed you will find a blank to be filled out, and a return envelope. The money can be sent in the form of stamps, cash, money order or check. You will receive prompt receipt from our Treasurer.

Please let us hear from you at once.

Yours very truly,

Booker T. Washington

Principal.

*John C. Van Dyke duck hunting in Maryland in the 1890s.*

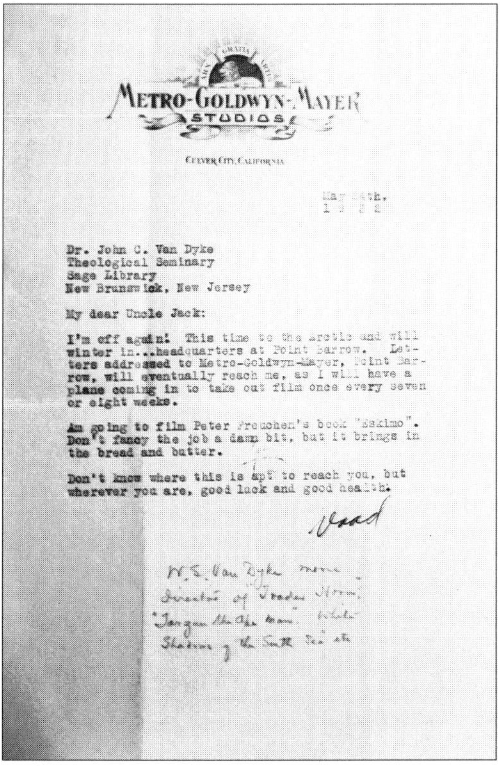

METRO-GOLDWYN-MAYER STUDIOS

CULVER CITY, CALIFORNIA

May 24th,
1932

Dr. John C. Van Dyke
Theological Seminary
Sage Library
New Brunswick, New Jersey

My dear Uncle Jack:

I'm off again! This time to the Arctic and will winter in...headquarters at Point Barrow. Letters addressed to Metro-Goldwyn-Mayer, Point Barrow, will eventually reach me, as I will have a plane coming in to take out film once every seven or eight weeks.

Am going to film Peter Freuchen's book "Eskimo". Don't fancy the job a damn bit, but it brings in the bread and butter.

Don't know where this is apt to reach you, but wherever you are, good luck and good health!

Woody

W. S. Van Dyke movie director of "Trader Horn," "Tarzan the Ape Man," "White Shadows of the South Sea" etc

*Letter to John C. Van Dyke from his nephew Woodbridge Strong Van Dyke.*

# *The Letters*

## PRINCETON UNIVERSITY
### *Charles Scribner's Sons Archives**

*Del Rio, Texas*
*May 23, 1901*

Dear Brownell,

I am sending you by ["Express" marked out, replaced by] registered mail today a book manuscript on the "Desert." Take a look at it, please, and tell me if the Scribners want it. They will have to take it anyway, for they published the first book in the series, *Nature for Its Own Sake.*[1] This [*The Desert*] is the *Second Studies in Natural Appearances.*[2] It's a whole lot better than the swash which today is being turned out as "literature." And it will sell, too; but not up in the hundreds of thousands. It is not so bad as that. My audience is only a few thousand, thank God.

If the Scribners want it (same terms as the "Nature" book), have it sent to the printers as incl.[3] The page type, style, etc. should follow the first book in every respect. There is only one illustration—a frontispiece. You will find the photograph for it between the sheets of the magazine enclosed with manuscript. Look out for this photograph, for it can't be replaced. The book will make about 230 or 250 pages, like the "Nature" book.

Expect to arrive in New Brunswick June 15, and if proof can be got together for me at that time, so much the better. Expect also to remain in Jersey all summer. But the climate may not agree, and I may have to emigrate again. That is why I want to get along with the proofs as fast as possible. Proofreading in Mexico with the *Police Gazette* for reference library is unsatisfactory. Feeling pretty well and shall be mighty glad to see somebody again. Send

---

* Courtesy of Charles Scribner III, Charles Scribner's Sons Archives. All letters in the Charles Scribner's Sons Archives, the Henry Van Dyke Family Papers, and the Harrison S. Morris Papers courtesy of the Manuscripts Division, Department of Rare Books and Special Collections, Princeton University Library. Published with permission. Hereafter cited as Princeton University Library. All letters in the Scribner's Archives are located in Author Files I, Box 160, Van Dyke Folders 1/2.

me a line here (Del Rio, Texas) if you get the manuscript all right. Shall probably stay here until about June 12th.

Yours hastily,
John C. Van Dyke

W. C. Brownell

• • •

1. The series of books Van Dyke mentions consists of six volumes written over the decades. After the general thesis statement of *Nature for Its Own Sake* (1898), volumes thereafter treat the aesthetics of particular natural features of the earth, as indicated by their titles: *The Desert* (1901), *The Opal Sea* (1906), *The Mountain* (1916), *The Grand Canyon* (1920), and *The Meadows* (1926). See Wild, "A Western Sun Sets in the East: The Five 'Appearances' Surrounding John C. Van Dyke's *The Desert.*"

2. As printed, the subtitle of *The Desert* substitutes *Further* for *Second.*

3. Though we do not have royalty information for the book mentioned, *Nature for Its Own Sake,* the several contracts appearing at the beginning of the Princeton correspondence with Scribner's indicate that Van Dyke usually received a royalty of 15 percent, based on the retail price. The contracts mention no advance.

*Del Rio, Texas*
*June 4 [1901]*

Dear Brownell,

I have your letter of May 31 about the "Desert" book. You understand, I suppose, that the proofs are to be sent to New Brunswick, where I hope to be in a few days or so. I wish you would read the galley proofs and give me the benefit of your suggestions. I haven't lost any idiocies since I have been out here, and I surely must have picked up a lot of mannerisms. I'm relying on you to keep me from making too big an ass of myself. I'm not likely to get at the proofs before the 20th.

Thanks for your good wishes about my health. I've gotten to be such a crank that I don't know whether I am sick or well, but if you could hear me you would probably think me dying. But I haven't gotten to that pass.

Yours ever,
John C. Van Dyke

*September 9, 1901*

Dear Brownell,

[The letter begins with two paragraphs of discussion, mostly illegible, concerning a misquote in Brownell's *French Art.*]

I saw the Desert book today. Don't like the color of the cover. My taste was bad. Better go back to the apple green of the *Nature for Its Own Sake* when a new batch is formed up.[4]

Yours very briefly,
John C. Van Dyke

• • •

4. Published in September of 1901, the initial edition of *The Desert* bore the title and an abstract flower stamped in gold on a medium-brown cover. Given the handsome edition, one puzzles over Van Dyke's grumpy response. To have said "My taste was bad" is a singular event in Van Dyke's life.

THE PRESBYTERIAN HOSPITAL
In the City of New York
70th Street & Madison Avenue

*14th May [1898—misdated; 1902?]*

Dear Brownell,

Here is a letter from my California brother—about "The Desert."[5] There may be something in what he says because I have heard nothing from Los Angeles. At Tucson, the Bookman reports it as one of the best selling books. There should be some special effort made at Phoenix, El Paso, Los Angeles, San Bernardino, Pasadena, and other California towns.[6]

Dr. McCash cut the appendix out of me here in the hospital a couple of weeks ago. Since then I have been growing together again. Am to go home on Saturday of this week. The pain wasn't much, but I don't like this lying on my back like a sea turtle in a fish market. McCash says I have had chronic appendicitis for a long time and that I will now be a new man. I hope to the Lord he is right, but I'm a little skeptical all the same.[7]

John C. Van Dyke

• • •

5. The letter from Theodore Strong Van Dyke is not extant.

6. Because of transportation difficulties and the relatively small population in the western United States, publishers of the time, concentrated in the East, tended to make light of markets beyond the Mississippi. See, for instance, Karen S. Langlois's "Mary Austin and Houghton Mifflin Company."

7. Illness and depression dogged Van Dyke long after his return from the desert. The removal of his appendix did not help. Worse, in the hospital he developed postoperative pneumonia (Van Dyke, *Autobiography* 125).

GARDNER A. SAGE LIBRARY
Theological Seminary
Reformed Church in America
New Brunswick, N.J.

*June 2 [1902 or 1903]*

Dear Brownell,

Font galleys returned by mail. Also "The conventionalized cactus." It certainly is not a realized cactus, but it will do. Reduction in size will improve it.[8]

Beginning with Thursday of this week, will you kindly send proof to me c/o John N. Conyughau of Wilkes-Barre, Pa? The heat is infernal and I want to get out fast.

Do you know Seymour Eaton's scheme of the Book Lovers Library at Phila? He has baited me with a $25 check to give him the titles of three books on art for circulation in their reading courses.

I have named:

Fromentin, Old Masters, etc.
Stillman, Old Italian Masters
Brownell's French Art

I hope he will buy an edition of each, but he probably will not.

Yours,
JCVD

• • •

8. In 1902 or 1903 Scribner's issued a slightly revised edition of *The Desert*. Also around this time, possibly at the same time, the publisher changed the gold flower stamped on the cover of *The Desert* to a gold saguaro cactus. The tangled publishing history of the book, together with

lack of editions in their original bindings, prevents a precise fix on the dates of the changes.

*El Monte, Cal.*
*April 20, 1915*

Chas. Scribner's Sons
New York

Sirs:

I venture to write to make a suggestion that very likely may not be acceptable, but on the possibility that it may. The well-known pecuniary disabilities of authors as a class must be my excuse.

It has occurred to me that you might be disposed to consider issuing a more fully illustrated edition of Dr. Van Dyke's classic *The Desert* than the one now published with frontispiece only. In that case, I happen to be in a position to take just such photographs as you would require. I am on an extended horseback journey in the Colorado Desert preparing a book of travel and description (such as my *California Coast Trails* and *Yosemite Trails* [Houghton Mifflin Co., 1913, 1911])—{parentheses and brackets in original}. I am securing a great number of very intriguing photographs, only a small number of which will find place in the projected volume. I shall therefore have very many good photographs that would be excellent to illustrate the text of *The Desert*, and I should be very glad in case you like the idea to have them so used. I shall probably have well over a hundred unique, or at least very interesting, desert pictures when I complete my circuit of the region—more than sufficient for the needs of both volumes without any conflict. I will also say, further, that I fancy many readers must be of my opinion that a book of the character of Professor Van Dyke's might with great advantage be fully illustrated.

In case you would like to commission me to supply a number of such photographs as I have suggested, I should be much pleased to hear from you. I would indicate the consideration of $100 for say fifteen or twenty as being reasonable in my view—the negatives to become your property, of course.

Possibly the suggestion should be made to the author instead of the publisher, but in that case you will no doubt take it up with him. Awaiting the favor of your reply at convenience. I am

Yours very truly,
J. Smeaton Chase[9]

• • •

9. In this and following letters, writer and photographer J. Smeaton Chase (1864–1923) need not have sounded such a supplicant. An Englishman and amateur naturalist of considerable substance, he wandered on horseback up and down the West Coast, and by the end of the year of this letter had several fine books about the region to his credit.

RUTGERS COLLEGE
New Brunswick, New Jersey

*September 2, 1915*

Chas. Scribner's Sons

Dear Sirs:

Thank you for the check for enclosed account which came in and was deposited during my absence in the west.[10]

Three items require rectification. The "London, Munich, and Berlin" are issued at $1.00 and not 75¢. The same error occurred in the last account and probably your book keeper is harking back to his original error. It is a small matter but it may as well be corrected.[11]

Yours very truly,
John C. Van Dyke

• • •

10. Though the exact dates of Van Dyke's comings and goings cannot always be determined, over the years he traveled a great deal in the American West. He visited a brother in Oregon, spent a number of summers at the Grand Canyon, and on an unknown number of occasions returned to Theodore's ranch on the Mojave Desert. On this last score, for instance, a Van Dyke relative owns a series of photographs taken at the ranch, showing Van Dyke at various ages. See the portfolio of photos in Van Dyke's *Autobiography* (following 127).

11. There's far more going on here than meets the eye.

This is not simply a writer turning picky and demanding correction of a minor mistake in his royalty statement, with the publisher graciously responding in the following letter. Rather, it shows how downright self-absorbed and impossible Van Dyke could get. The book referred to is part of a series, New Guides to Old Masters, a multivolume series of guides to Europe's art museums. As fate would have it, most of the books were issued just as World War I broke out and therefore were, through no one's fault, a huge financial disaster for Scribner's. Van Dyke's *Autobiography* shows the depth of his disappointment over the loss (155–57).

However, by next demanding the pittance from an already failed project, a sulking Van Dyke is really pushing his luck with Scribner's. Their courteous response shows how far they were willing to tolerate Van Dyke's childish bouts in hopes of reaping profits from his future books.

Despite this passing tiff, Van Dyke was quick to realize the change in the book market resulting from the Great War. With tourism cut off to Europe, he shifted geographical gears and once again turned his writing attention to the American West (*Autobiography* 167–72).

[typewritten]

*September 3, 1915*

Professor John C. Van Dyke
Rutgers College
New Brunswick, N.J.

Dear Sir:

We are in receipt of your favor of the 2nd inst. enclosing our royalty report of August 2nd, and in reply enclose a corrected report. The difference, $1.65, has been credited to your account, and will be included in our next statement, February 1st. We regret exceedingly that these mistakes should have put you to any trouble.

Yours truly,
[signature illegible]

[typewritten]

*September 17, 1917*

Dear Professor Van Dyke:

Mr. J. Smeaton Chase, who has written two or three books, has just called with an extensive collection of photographs of the desert and suggests the possibility of using some of them to make an illustrated edition of your book. He is coming in again

Thursday morning, between ten and eleven, and I suggest that if convenient you might be here at that time to look over them and to consider with us the desirability of possibly making use of any of them.

Please send me a line to assure us of your receipt of this and to let us know whether it will be convenient for you to be here at that time. Mr. Chase expects to leave town on Friday.

Very sincerely yours,
A. H. S. [Arthur H. Scribner]

To Professor John C. Van Dyke

[typewritten]

RUTGERS COLLEGE
New Brunswick, New Jersey

*September 18, 1917*

Mr. Arthur H. Scribner
5th Ave. at 48th St., New York

Dear Mr. Scribner:

In California this summer I heard so much in praise of my desert book that I had determined to suggest to you on my return the possibility of an illustrated edition; but your letter of this morning happily forestalls me. I think the popularity of the book warrants an illustrated edition, and I shall be glad to prepare one. Mr. Chase, with his collection of photographs of the desert, has dropped out of the sky most opportunely. I am much interested to find out what he has because I have very little or nothing. About coming in on Thursday, I doubt that it is possible because I have a lecture on hand, but do not let Mr. Chase get away with his photographs, for we need them. Could they perhaps be sent to me here to look over quietly? Or I might come in Friday morning between ten and eleven.

Yours very truly,
John C. Van Dyke

[handwritten in lower margin:] 10:30 Friday

[typewritten]

RUTGERS COLLEGE
New Brunswick, New Jersey

*October 4, 1917*

Mr. Arthur Scribner
Chas. Scribner's Sons
5th Avenue at 48th St., New York

My dear Mr. Scribner:

I saw Mr. Chase last night at the Century Club and went over the photographs to illustrate the Desert book. I selected thirty-two as you suggested, and Mr. Chase will report them to you. In addition to these I have six photographs of my own that perhaps can be added.

I will come in and see you about the whole matter the first of next week if that is convenient for you.

Yours very truly,
John C. Van Dyke

MR. ARTHUR SCRIBNER
5th Ave. at 48th St., New York

*October 9, 1917*

My Dear Mr. Scribner:

I find that I shall not be able to see you this week regarding Mr. Chase's photographs for the Desert book. However, there is not very much to say about it, and if you have the photographs in hand, could you not have them made up in half-tones without further delay? I send enclosed six photographs that I should like added to the thirty-two selected from Mr. Chase, but if that is too many they can be left out.

Proofs of the plates could be sent me, and I can arrange their placing in the book. A copy of the plates should also be sent to Mr. Chase, who will affix the proper titles to them.

Yours very truly,
John C. Van Dyke

*October 18, 1917*

Dear Professor Van Dyke:

Mr. Chase called and told us that he would not be able to supply the thirty-two negatives selected for your book *The Desert* until, I think he said, the last of this month. This did not seem to me material as we had thought that it was better not to publish the illustrated edition until shortly after the first of the year. Your first thought may be otherwise, it being an illustrated book and having perhaps some holiday appeal, but all our announcements, of course, have been widely distributed some time since, and the booksellers have all their supply of such books, so that it would be difficult to secure their cooperation. If published early in the year, it will not be swamped by so many other books of holiday nature, of which announcements have been in their hands for some months, and our own belief is that it will receive much better attention at that time and also be in season to appeal to those who are about to take a trip to the Pacific Coast. A considerable portion of the sale should be on the Coast itself, and even if the book were rushed through under the most favorable auspices, it could not be shipped in time to reach the Coast in season to catch the holiday trade there.

Thirty-two plates were as many as we had anticipated, but when the other negatives are received and the estimates completed, we can then decide perhaps just how essential the additional ones may be.

Yours very truly,
A. H. S.

To Professor John C. Van Dyke

PALM SPRINGS, CALIFORNIA

*November 7, 1917*

Messrs. Chas. Scribner's Sons
New York, New York

Dear Sirs:

With this I send the 32 negatives chosen by Professor Van Dyke recently, in accordance with the arrangement made among

Mr. Scribner, Mr. Van Dyke, and the writer to illustrate *The Desert.* I have also enclosed a sort of memorandum bill, on the basis agreed between Mr. Scribner and me.

I hardly need to hope that your photographic department will secure the best results in making the prints from these negatives, but prints that I had made by Underwood and Underwood, who are supposed to be experts in the line, proved so far inferior to prints made here from the same negatives that I venture to offer the hint. Every one of these negatives will yield a quite excellent print; but *Velox* paper should be used and no other. On the envelope enclosing each negative I have written full data for Mr. Van Dyke's information in citing the picture for his book. I have not myself, except in one instance, suggested a title, but have only given the material for it. I shall be very glad to furnish any further data that you or he may desire.

The Chapter numbers marked on the envelope are according to Mr. Van Dyke's arrangement.

I would draw your attention to the fact that two of the pictures have been published before—that of the roadrunner in a little child's paper called *The Schoolmate* and the one I have called "Sunset and the Sentinel," in *St. Nicholas.* Mr. Van Dyke considered this no drawback to his use of them, but I wish you to be aware of the fact, though no doubt immaterial.

You will, I feel sure, be quite willing that my name appear as having furnished the illustrations for the new edition of *The Desert.* Mr. Van Dyke thought I could take it for granted that "credit" would be thus given: "Illustrated from photographs by J. Smeaton Chase," or some similar formula. Will you very kindly advise me on the point?[12]

With appreciation of your courtesy, and my personal compliments to Mr. Scribner, I am,

Yours faithfully,<br>
J. Smeaton Chase

· · ·

12. Mr. Chase's wish was granted. The title page includes the notice: "With Illustrations from Photographs by J. Smeaton Chase."

*November 27, 1917*

Dear Mr. Van Dyke:

We have now received from Mr. Chase the originals of the illustrations for *The Desert* and have prints of these which we can send to you for you to designate the titles and place the illustrations, or if you will drop in, we can go over at the same time any details that may occur to you, showing you the proposed size of book, etc.

Thirty-two is as many illustrations as we can well afford, but you may wish to substitute your own for some of Mr. Chase's. As a whole, these look to me very attractive, and I hope the book in this form will do well.[13]

It is quite customary with us to make a different arrangement as to royalty on illustrated editions similar to this, and we hope that you will be content with ten percent in this edition, the royalty on your other edition of course not to be changed. We find that the negatives alone, with their reproduction and other minor charges, mount up to over four hundred dollars, and other costs of manufacture are, as you know much higher at present than ever before.

I am,

Very sincerely yours,
A. H. S.

To Professor John C. Van Dyke

• • •

13. Although sales figures are not available, apparently the edition did well. After the illustrated edition of *The Desert* appeared in 1918, most subsequent reprints of the book during Van Dyke's lifetime contained Chase's photographs.

RUTGERS COLLEGE
New Brunswick, New Jersey

*November 28, 1917*

Arthur H. Scribner, Esq.
5th Ave. at 48th Street
New York, New York

Dear Mr. Scribner:

Will you kindly send me out the prints of Mr. Chase's originals for *The Desert*, and I will arrange them at my leisure out here? I can come in later and have a talk about the details of the book.

All right about the matter of royalty on the illustrated edition.

Yours very truly,
John C. Van Dyke

[handwritten in left margin:] 10 percent instead of 15 percent on this edition.

*January 4, 1918*

Dear Van Dyke:

We should like to have you agree with us that the book-plate entitled "Books by Professor John C. Van Dyke" be omitted from the new edition of *The Desert*, with whose new and "different" character it's rather markedly commercial, and advertising aspect does not seem to us quite to accord. Kindly drop a line addressed to the house as soon as convenient, as the manufacturing department needs to move as soon as possible.

Sincerely yours,
W. C. Brownell

To Professor John C. Van Dyke

RUTGERS COLLEGE
New Brunswick, New Jersey

*January 5, 1918*

Charles Scribner's Sons
5th Ave. at 48th St.
New York

Dear Sirs:

I quite agree with the suggestion of Mr. Brownell that the book-plate entitled "Books by John C. Van Dyke" be omitted from the new edition of *The Desert.*

Yours very truly,
John C. Van Dyke

*February 18, 1918*

Dear Van Dyke:

We are sending you two copies of the illustrated *Desert.* Do you see any flies on it? Any there may be have escaped me, and I feel like recording my opinion that congratulations are due all around.

Sincerely yours,
W. C. B.

To Professor John C. Van Dyke

PALM SPRINGS
Riverside County, California

*March 19, 1918*

Chas. Scribner's Sons Company
New York
Mr. Maxwell Perkins

My Dear Sir:

I notice by an advertisement in the *New York Times Book Review* that the new illustrated edition of *The Desert* is on the market. I don't know whether I may be asking something inconsistent with the rules of your House, but I should be very glad, supposing it is allowable, if you would be so kind as to send me eight copies for my own use and for giving to friends, at the wholesale price. If it cannot be done, I must deny myself the pleasure of dispensing volumes so freely; but perhaps you may think it allowable to stretch the author's privilege in this case so as to cover the humble auxiliary illustrator.

If you can send them, I will remit at once a receipt of the bill—in advance of the books if you prefer.

With kind remembrances, I am,

Yours very truly,
J. Smeaton Chase

P.S.

"Palm Springs" is the postal address; but for express packages "Whitewater, Cal."

*March 27, 1918*

Dear Mr. Chase:

If you have not received any copies of the new edition of *The Desert*, it was wholly through an error, as we intended to send you two, and we take pleasure in doing so now. We are also sending you six others, which we are charging under the same discount that we allow authors. We hope you will be pleased with the appearance of the edition. We are very much so ourselves and expect it to do well.

P

To J. Smeaton Chase, Esq.

EL TOVAR GRAND CANYON ARIZONA

*July 5, 1919*

Dear Brownell:

I am returning the last of the galley proofs today [of *The Grand Canyon*] [14] and have also corrected and returned about a third of the page proofs. Thank you again many times for reading the proof. You have kept me out of personal flippancies and I know not how many irrelevancies. I wish the book were [three illegible words]. I always feel sad when I see the thesis in type.

The Santa Fe and Fred Harvey people seem very much pleased that I am doing a Canyon book. The office heads at Chicago and Kansas City have written me offering me all their photographs for illustration. They have many thousands. They all seem to have read *The Desert*, and the Fred Harvey people have been handling it on their newsstands for years. They will handle the Canyon book with a greater interest. Hope you are well.[15]

Yours ever,
John C. Van Dyke

• • •

14. John C. Van Dyke, *The Grand Canyon of the Colorado: Recurrent Studies in Impressions and Appearances* (1920). Van Dyke leads his readers to believe that during his summers at the Grand Canyon he explored its labyrinths through heroic feats of hiking (*Autobiography* 170–71). This is more literary smoke. While regaling himself with the beauty of the Canyon, Van Dyke was enjoying the elegant comforts of the El Tovar Hotel, on whose letterhead he writes to Brownell (Wild and Carmony 73). See Ayer's reminiscence of Van Dyke at the Grand Canyon, Newberry Library section, below.

15. The handling of *The Grand Canyon* by railroad concessionaire Fred Harvey was a big boon for the book, as sales figures in the next letter bear out. In light of this, it is curious that *The Grand Canyon* only went through two reprintings in Van Dyke's lifetime. Thereafter, perhaps the dampened travel of the Great Depression caused the book to languish. It is now again in print.

*June 29, 1920*

Dear Mr. Van Dyke:

We had several conversations about the use of your *Grand Canyon* by Harvey, so I write at once to let you know that, in addition to a couple of previous smaller orders, we have now secured from him, after some correspondence and the quoting of a special price, an order for 1,000 copies, 500 of these to be shipped at once and the balance to be held and charged in October. Altogether, with these orders and the natural sale, the book is making a good showing.

Very sincerely yours,
A. H. S.

To Professor John C. Van Dyke

HOTEL WASHINGTON
Cristobal, C.Z.

*January 7, 1926*

Dear Brownell,[16]

*Know ye the land where the parrot and monkey*
*Are emblems of things that are done in their clime,*
*Where the howl of the dog and the bray of the donkey*
*Lift high in their discord and madden to crime?*

Well, (with apologies to Goethe and Byron) this is it![17] Color belonging to the Panama Republic and the rummiest town extant! A real nigger nest where they sell parrots and monkeys in the street, and everything forbidden by the decalogue and decent municipal government on the inside of the houses. But right next to it, just across the railway bed, is Cristobal, controlled by the United States—a model of cleanliness and decency. Every American chest (and there are plenty of them here) swells with pride over it. As for the Canal, even the bark-bound Jamaican Britishers admit that there the United States set a pattern for the world.

Jamaica, where I stopped for four weeks, is very picturesque. I got three chapters of a new book out of it. The book will probably be some sort of study in tropic seas, light, color, etc.

Panama not a swamp with alligators, snakes and stagnant water but a pass in the sierra cut by the Chagres River which the Canal follows! Where do we get these ridiculous preconceptions! The coast all around the Caribbean is mountainous except just as you enter the Canal.

Going through the Canal tomorrow and down the coast to Valparaiso on the SS "Ebro." A wire here this morning says there is fighting on between Chile and Peru. I'll probably get there in time to get shot in the stomach but I shall sail on scheduled time just the same.

Two weeks to Valparaiso! Distances are long and mails very slow. I'll send you an address later and perhaps you can send me a copy of the Meadows book. The only address I can now give is c/o Anglo South American Bank, Santiago, Chile, but a letter to reach me there should leave New York by Jan. 20.

Hope the New Year opens up happily for you and will continue propitious. I seem to be very well and thrive on heat.

Regards and good luck,
John C. Van Dyke

• • •

16. Here, Van Dyke's handwriting changes, racing across the pages and reflecting the letter's manic flight.

17. Van Dyke's apologies are in order. A source for his verse is Goethe's popular and evocative poem "Mignon." It begins, "Kennst Du das Land, wo die Zitronen blühen . . . ?" (Do you know the land where lemons blossom . . . ?)

However, more influential on Van Dyke's tone here is

> Know ye the land where the cypress and myrtle
> Are emblems of deeds that are done in their clime?
> Where the rage of the vulture, the love of the turtle,
> Now melt into sorrow, now madden to crime?
> (Lord Byron, *The Bride of Abydos*, Canto I, lines 1–4)

## *Henry Van Dyke Family Papers**

THEOLOGICAL SEMINARY
New Brunswick
New Jersey

*November 10, 1893*

My dear Cousin:[18]

Are your engagements and your temper such that you could be induced to make a ten or fifteen minute talk before the friends and officers of the Women's Depository,[19] which holds its annual meeting at Mrs. H. O. Arman's, 67th St. and 5th Ave. on Dec. 12 at 8:30 p.m.? The first part of the evening is devoted to reports by the Depository officers, then there is Music, recitation,

* Manuscripts Division, Department of Rare Books and Special Collections, Princeton University Library. Published with permission of the Princeton University Library.

etc.; and then they like to have some bright man say "something nice" about Women's Depositories in general and this one in particular, together with the incidental treasures one may log up in Heaven by depositing certain sums with the present society. I believe the home of this society is the "Morrison Ave. Exchange for Women's Work." Dr. Hall was the duck making service for them last year, and may have an "awful eye" fixed on you for this year. I promised Mrs. J. Hoodwright that I would at least lay the matter before you.

This is the penalty of greatness. You shouldn't be such a "Spell-binder." Seriously, if you are disposed to do them this favor you would not find it anything of a task. You know the caliber of that fashionable society that interests itself in charitable undertakings. It is not severely critical. If you will go, I will go along with you and sprinkle as many roses in your path as possible.

President Eliot inquired for you the other night, but I was not able to tell him much about you.[20] Hope you are feeling better than when I last saw you. Don't be discouraged: this wave of nervous despondency which seems to be rolling over all of us just now is sure to recede. Last winter I thought it never would but now that my nose is getting above water I feel better. Everything passes.

Yours very truly,
John C. Van Dyke

• • •

18. Box 134, Folder 11, Henry Van Dyke Papers, Princeton University Library. Poet, Presbyterian minister, professor of English at Princeton University, and a fisherman who wrote outdoor essays with classic purity, cousin Henry van Dyke (1852–1933) was one of the nation's cultural icons. In 1913, President Wilson appointed van Dyke United States minister to the Netherlands and Luxembourg. However, unable to reconcile his support of the Allies during World War I with his government's neutrality at the time, he resigned the post in 1916.

19. Apparently, "Ladies' Depository" was the actual name. According to its *Annual Report* of 1847, the organization was founded in 1833 "for the purpose of supplying work to respectable females of every religious denomination."

20. Charles William Eliot, president of Harvard University from 1869 to 1909.

*New Brunswick, N.J.*
*December 22, 1914*

Dear Cousin Henry:

I am writing this note of introduction for Mr. Walter S. Thomson, a nephew of the late Frank Thomson of the Pennsylvania Railroad. All the Thomsons are old and dear friends of mine and any consideration you can show to any one of them will be greatly appreciated by me.

Hope you are to have as Merry a Christmas as the unfortunate circumstances will permit of. Keep well; and more power to your elbow. We are all proud of your doings.

Yours ever,
John C. Van Dyke

Hon. Henry Van Dyke
United States Minister
The Hague
Holland

[typewritten]

*The Hague, Netherlands*
*May 19, 1916*

My dear Cousin John:

This is just a line to thank you for sending me your charming book "The Raritan." I like your ideas of linking the story of our family with the little river.

I think that some of the conjectural dates given in your book are not quite right, and I am inclined to believe that the family never really lived in the city of Amsterdam, but came either from the island of Texel, or perhaps from the region of Harlingen, in Friesland.[21] It has been thus far extremely difficult to get any definite traces in regard to the question. But after all, what does it matter? It remains certain that they loved the out-of-doors, and continued to love it, and still love it, as you have shown in your books on the desert, the sea, and the mountains.

Meantime, I am toiling at the mill with questions about spinach seed, sugar beet seed, coffee, dyestuffs, gasoline, imports of gold, commercial treaties, and so forth. Pity and respect me!

Cordially yours,
[signature not legible]

Mr. John C. Van Dyke
New Brunswick, N.J.

• • •

21. The previous December 22, 1914, letter and this May 19, 1916, letter are located in Box 76, Folder 5, Henry Van Dyke Papers, Princeton University Library. Cavalier John C. Van Dyke often badly botches his dates. In the endpaper of his family history, *The Raritan*, he even got the birthdate of his favorite brother, Theodore, wrong. For a more extensive history of the Van Dykes, see Aitken.

## ARIZONA HISTORICAL SOCIETY
## *Robert H. Forbes Papers**

RUTGERS COLLEGE
and
RUTGERS SCIENTIFIC SCHOOL
The New Jersey State College for the
Benefit of Agriculture and the Mechanic Arts
New Brunswick, N.J.

*November 4, 1901*

My Dear Professor Forbes:

I have your letter of October 27th about the desert book. I am glad if it has appealed to you in any of its chapters. I do not count it "the only greatest effort of my life." It's the book of a sick man written to escape morbid mental anatomy and with considerable of the morbidity sticking to its pages. And blunders of course! I am always very careful of my facts and yet in every book there are half a dozen very stupid blunders. In my *Nature for Its Own Sake* I discovered the day after publication that I had told my

* Robert H. Forbes Papers, MS 261, Box 12, f. 11. Arizona Historical Society, Tucson.

audience that Mont Blanc was "some *five* miles high," when every idiot in an asylum knows better. Why is it that we occasionally write "1892" when we mean "1492"? The "purple" flower of the sahuaro is another case to the point. I must have seen them thousands of times yet I got it down "purple" in my notes. Such things are sheer stupidity—mental lapses. At other times I am misled by "authorities." I had the spread of the condor's wings at nine feet and his weight at 25 pounds, but a California ornithologist wrote it down so positively as "sometimes fifteen feet and forty pounds in weight" that I followed his lead and blundered again. The newness of the subject in book form was also a little disconcerting. No one had gone into the details or tried to put the material together; and no one, except yourself and Professor Blake—no one in that whole desert country—knew a blessed thing about desert plants, animals, rocks, or skies. In Mexico I sometimes had to ask twenty people the same question and then guess at the right answer. I asked you so many questions that finally I was ashamed to ask any more. And I never planned it as a scientific book. I was anxious only that I should get the exact facts for literary purposes.

Have you told me in your letter *all* the blunders that you found? I ask because I am correcting for a new edition. About the legend of the Cocopa [Indians] concerning the recession of the Salton Sea I am almost certain it was Professor Blake who told me there was no legend. But perhaps I was wrong. Do you suppose he would mind if I should quote him in a footnote that there *is* a legend?

About the desert flowers—the penstemons, poppies, lupines, etc.—are you not thinking of them about Tucson? I say p. 147 "Many tales are told of the flowers that grow on the waste after the rains, but I have not seen them though I have seen the rains" and at the end of the paragraph: "Higher up in the hills and along the mesas one often meets with many strange flowers . . . *but not down in the hot valleys of the desert.*" If you have seen the poppies and penstemons "by the square mile" down in the lower valleys or the Salton Basin, I should be very glad to quote you about it. And I would like to quote you in that horned toad story, but I wouldn't stand sponsor for it myself. I never heard it, but it is surely "a snake story" of the first quality. I have heard of the horned toad spitting blood in your or your dog's eyes and producing blindness, but I failed to verify it, though I gave the toad many chances to do this celebrated act.

Believe me, I am greatly obliged to you for calling my attention to these matters, and if you will help me out with further corrections, I shall be under still greater obligations. The little book is favorably received in this part of the country and is likely to run through several editions; therefore, it should not give misinformation.

I may be out in Arizona again before long. I am neither very well nor very ill—just morbid, uneasy, dissatisfied—like a steer in a box car. My plans are for the West Indies or Egypt next month, but I may make it Mexico again.

My regards to you and to Professor Blake. I have memories of pleasant chats with you both.

Yours very truly,
John C. Van Dyke

Professor R. H. Forbes
Tucson

## NEWBERRY LIBRARY
### *Morton Payne Papers*[*]

RUTGERS COLLEGE
and
RUTGERS SCIENTIFIC SCHOOL
The New Jersey State College for the
Benefit of Agriculture and the Mechanic Arts
New Brunswick, N.J.

*January 12, 1897*

Dear Mr. Payne:

I have just sent you a telegram saying to make the date of January 29 for the Twentieth Century Club. There will be no

* The Morton Payne Papers, The Newberry Library Archives, the Newberry Library.

trouble about my keeping the engagement, tho to do so I shall have to change a date at Paterson. That I think can be done easily enough. At any rate, presume on January 29, unless I telegraph to the contrary Friday morning of this week.

I shall come on the PRR limited and get in Chicago Friday morning, leaving there at 11:30 the same night for N.Y. I presume your lecture is called for 8 p.m. and any reception that may follow will certainly be over before 11:30 p.m.

Have a lantern sheet, operator, and pointer for me, please. Also, a reading desk, or pulpit, or table with box on it. I don't want one of those one-legged skeleton lecterns to read from. I shall read little and talk more, but I always want something substantial before me. The subject, you understand, is to be "Portrait Painting," illustrated by slides of many celebrated portraits.

I shall be glad if you will let me know the place of holding the lecture and also the usual audience (in numbers) that you have.

Yours very truly,
John C. Van Dyke

Wm. M. Payne
1601 Prairie Av.
Chicago

## *Edward Everett Ayer Papers**

*Following is a selection from the journal of Edward Everett Ayer recounting a 1918 stay at the El Tovar hotel, perched elegantly on the rim of the Grand Canyon. Ayer had, by this time, made his fortune in the cross-tie business and become a noted antiquarian, having served, for instance, as first president of the Field Museum of Natural History in Chicago. Ayer had first traveled through the Southwest as part of Major Fergusson's California Column in 1862. He had noted in a letter to Van Dyke (included in the Sage Library collection, pp. 132–33) two years before he made this entry that the desert had not only affected him pro-*

* The Edward Everett Ayer Papers, The Newberry Library Archives, the Newberry Library.

*foundly but had also hit home with his friend Benjamin Winchell, "Vice President and Traffic Manager of the Union Pacific."*

[typewritten]

. . . also looking down upon the mouth and the canyon of the Little Colorado which comes from the south and up the remarkable canyon of the Grand Canyon, which there trends to the north—all the great plain with Cedar Mountain in the immediate foreground, and Navajo Mountain in the far distance, and all the intervening spaces, with magnificent colors also represented in the stones in the canyon, making its name, Painted Desert, most appropriate. It was a wonderful trip and a wonderful view.

When we returned to the hotel that night, who should we find there but J.C. Van Dyke, a gentleman that Mrs. Ayer and I are more indebted to than any other man in the world, for our knowledge of the desert, the mountain and the sea, and also largely so, too, for his wonderful books on art. In natural history he has written "The Desert," describing every phase of it for every hour of the day and night—how it was made, the struggle with all the plants that grow on it, the supreme struggle of all the animals that fly over it and live on it. In fact, I had been on the desert 30 years before I really had any idea of its grandeur or its beauty, and for the last 15 years in autoing Mrs. Ayer and I had rather be on the desert of Africa and America than any other place in the world in autoing. He has also written "The Mountain," which is equally fine, and "Nature for Nature's Sake [*sic*]," another book which combines more or less the studies of Natural History and Geology, and "The Opal Sea," another. I was somewhat familiar, having already a great library on ornithology, of the birds that fly over, and a little about the forests, and I crossed the ocean 35 times, intently looking at it all the time and wondering about it also, and I never really saw it until I had read J.C. Van Dyke's "The Opal Sea." He tells me that he is trying to prepare a book on the blue sky, and what a wonder it will be if he does.

I found Mr. Van Dyke at the hotel this night when we got back. I sent him my card. He dined with us that night and breakfasted with us the next morning. Then I took him out to the Painted Desert, visiting all these grand points of the Grand Canyon, and I had nearly ten hours with him that day, and you may readily believe me when I tell you that it was one of the most interesting ten hours I ever spent in my life.

## LIBRARY OF CONGRESS
### *Andrew Carnegie Papers**

*New Brunswick, N.J.*
*April 6 [1892?]*

Dear Mr. Carnegie:

I have ordered five of the pictures sent to your house. The other two I am afraid will not be ready for delivery before your departure on the 13th, in which case you will have to trust me for an accounting until your return.

The pictures have cost me some perplexity and trouble and I shall now insist upon your carrying out your part of the contract by "living with them" for a few weeks at least. They are all good pictures and if at the end of some weeks you still do not care for them why any dealer will give you more for them than they cost you. The frames alone should be worth nearly $300.

Of course you understand that any one of the pictures that does not please you in subject may be exchanged.

When the five are received will you please have your secretary notify me? I should like to run in and see if they are the goods as purchased.

Yours very truly,
John C. Van Dyke

Andrew Carnegie, Esq.

P.S.

I think to make my article for our Authors Club book on "What I Know about Picture Buying for Other People."

* Library of Congress, Manuscript Division. The ends of some of the letters to Carnegie in the Library of Congress bear brief remarks in shorthand, presumably notations by Carnegie's secretary. Because different shorthand systems were in use a century ago than prevail today, we were unable to find a specialist who could translate the notes.

*New Brunswick, N.J.*
*April 3, 1893*

My dear Mr. Carnegie:

The bronze has duly arrived, been "set up," and at present occupies a conspicuous place on my library table. It is certainly very good of you and Mrs. Carnegie to remember me in this way and I appreciate the kindness very much indeed—*only* if every time I give a two dollar and a half Madonna I am to receive a hundred dollar bronze I shan't feel much like giving away more Madonnas. However, I am selfish enough to keep this piece because it is very beautiful, and then, too, I like to think that Mr. and Mrs. Carnegie gave it to me. Did you know that the statuette was long considered—is so now—an avenging Diana with the bow in her hand after slaying the sons of Niobe? It is probably a Victory, but the shape of the head and the dress of the hair point to Diana.[22]

I have ordered another picture from Mr. Crane at $250 provided it suits, and he is delighted.[23] I told him exactly what you said, that the other picture was not paid enough for, and that pleased him more yet, though he confirmed what I told you, that he had only asked $140 for the first picture and that Potter Palmer *offered* $400 *for it probably because it was sold to me.*[24] The fact is that pictures are like Chatham Street Clothes—they have no market price. Crane has sold scores of pictures at $25 and $50 apiece. The Taker landscape which you have is a better picture than the Crane and yet only cost $150 *at catalogue price.* Mr. Chase asks for his smallest pictures from $200 to $500, yet I have one in my library that I bought at auction for $30, not because I wanted it but to save it from being sold at $15.[25] If the artists receive what they ask they will be more than satisfied. Some of them are high in price and some are low, dependent as much on the quantity produced as on the merit.

Did you find anything at the Academy that pleased you? There is likely to be better work at the Society which opens the middle of this month.

Thanking you again very much for the bronze and with regards to Mrs. Carnegie I am

Yours very truly,
John C. Van Dyke

• • •

22. The bronze is *Winged Victory*, a statue about 18 inches high, sculptor unknown. It is recorded in the holdings of the John C. Van Dyke collection of the Zimmerli Voorhees Museum at Rutgers. However, it went astray when loaned out years ago under a policy, since changed, for displaying the museum's art in various buildings around the campus (Telephone conversation, November 9, 1993, with Barbara Trelstad, registrar at the museum).

23. Bruce Crane (1857–1937) "was known particularly for scenes of Connecticut fields in autumnal grays and yellows" (see "Crane, Bruce," *Encyclopedia of American Art*). The John C. Van Dyke collection at the Voorhees Museum contains two untitled Crane canvases, a landscape and a marine scene.

24. Potter Palmer, a wealthy Chicago merchant and patron of the arts.

25. William Merritt Chase (1849–1916) was one of the preeminent artists of the Gilded Age. Here Van Dyke shows himself a deft buyer of art, for about this time Chase was on the rising curve of his reputation. Van Dyke prided himself in making such shrewd purchases ahead of the art market. Though Chase did not think of himself as a student of impressionism, he certainly was indebted to the movement. Himself quite a showman, Chase, along with Van Dyke, was a friend of the far more erumpent Whistler. For an overview and a selection of Chase's paintings, see Pisano, *William Merritt Chase*. The Chase portrait of Van Dyke used as the frontispiece of this book hangs in the Sage Library. For its strange role in following the intricacies of Van Dyke's life, see Wild, "Interviews and Notes."

*May 18, 1893*

My dear Mr. Carnegie:

Will you have your secretary send me word if the cabbage patch picture has been safely received?[26] I wish to send the painter a check for it but should like to know first that it has been delivered in good shape. It is far and away the best landscape I have yet obtained for you—in fact quite a capture. Hope you will be as well pleased with it as I am.

I shall be here any day that you and Mrs. Carnegie feel like coming out—only don't feel obliged to—come when you want to.

Yours very truly,
John C. Van Dyke

Andrew Carnegie, Esq.

• • •

26. An undated letter [1895] in the Smithsonian Institution, from Van Dyke to Mr. [William Nimick] Frew, a powerful attorney in Carnegie's

orbit, mentions the steel magnate's ownership of "A Cabbage Patch," by Joseph Boston.

However, that does not necessarily settle the issue. Given Van Dyke's long association with preeminent artist William M. Chase, a better-known picture, Chase's watercolor *The Potato Patch*, also is a likely candidate. Here, Van Dyke, who grew up romping across a countryside of woods and farms, is not confusing his vegetables. The reference to cabbage patch probably is humorous. "The specific subject of *The Potato Patch* is somewhat unusual for Chase, who is better known for depictions of upper-class leisure rather than the daily chores of the working class. This painting does demonstrate dashing style and interest in color, however, as well as Chase's ability to render any subject in an attractive way" (Pisano, *William Merritt Chase* 68). Pisano's next page reproduces the painting.

## *Joseph and Elizabeth Robins Pennell Collection**

RUTGERS COLLEGE
New Brunswick, New Jersey

*October 2, 1909*

Dear Pennell:

I have your letter with its "Kick" about the book, but the blamed thing is so much better than I had hoped for that I can't sympathize with you very much.[27] Those wavering borders, as I told you in London, I had not even noticed until you called my attention to them. It was then too late to do anything, for they had all been run off on the press. They certainly do not help the plates any but neither do they hurt them very much. The "peepul" will never see them. As for the title, I explained that in London. We enlarged the page and your title wouldn't fit the larger page. The elongated NEW YORK has been stretched to the breaking point and would go no farther. So the only thing to do was to set up the type title.

* Library of Congress, Manuscript Division. Born in Philadelphia, illustrator Joseph Pennell (1857–1926) spent much time living in London, where he and his wife Elizabeth befriended many artists, notably James McNeill Abbott Whistler.

You say nothing about the bully printing of the colored plates. Some of them I think are printed without the key black, or at least without any black ink. They look very decent I think. My "Kick" is that they chopped the margins off the pages, but that is counterbalanced by the publisher's Kick that they didn't want a book that would weigh a ton. But the book (as books go) is all right. The devil of it is that it isn't selling. Nothing doing. Everyone who thought to sell anything at the Fulton-Hudson show got left.[28] The saloons and the hotels got what there was. But the book will probably pull up later. The notices have been fairly good. The "Sun" took a kick at your paunch, which made me grin, and The Post cuffed me about over a column which will probably make you smile. Your friend Roweike I believe sends you clippings.

I saw the Keppel show yesterday. It looked very well and what is better they have sold for you about a hundred etchings, so they told me, but only about three or four of the New York drawings. So you see, you're in luck, if I am not.

The Fulton-Hudson row, with the exception of the military parade on Thursday, was about as fierce as anything I have seen. Tawdry, cheap, and correspondingly nasty. The "pageant" was a terror to gods and more, and the naval parade was disgraceful. The battleships were all right and looked well lying at anchor, but the procession was merely a collection of old brigs and river boats that wallowed along like empty pork barrels. The illumination of the city—especially the big bridges—was bully.

Will Low is either engaged or married to Mrs. Nice Manners, as you probably know by this time, so he probably won't come over to London for consolation.[29] I'm sorry Mrs. Pennell did not know that when she wrote. Naturally, it has caused some surprise over here.

But goodbye for the nonce. I'm busy with many things. Bronchitis about same. The air of God's country may have had something to do with the cure. Best regards to Mrs. Pennell. The McClellans send remembrances.[30]

Yours ever,
John C. Van Dyke

• • •

27. Published in the year of this letter and illustrated by Pennell, *The New New York* is a lovely book. A celebration of the city, its people, and culture, it happily violates many of Van Dyke's art tenets, among them that pristine nature, not the things of civilization, offers the best art. One guesses that with this volume Van Dyke was doing penance for his tirade of the year before, mending fences with the many people offended by his *Money God.*

28. In 1909 New York City combined the celebration of Henry Hudson's discovery of the Hudson River in 1609 with Robert Fulton's launching of his steamboat on the same river in 1807. As Van Dyke indicates here, with its military parades, flotillas, and blustery speeches, the Hudson-Fulton Fête was a grand and most fierce bash.

29. On November 4, 1909, American painter Will Low (1853–1932) married Mary Louise Fairchild. It was his second marriage.

30. Mr. and Mrs. George B. McClellan. An attorney, historian, and patron of the arts, Mr. McClellan served as a congressman and was the mayor of New York City at the time of this letter. He was the son of George Brinton McClellan Sr., a controversial Civil War general. Van Dyke and the McClellans were lifelong friends and sometime traveling companions (Van Dyke, *Autobiography* 71, 226–27 n. 7).

RUTGERS COLLEGE
and
RUTGERS SCIENTIFIC SCHOOL
The New Jersey State College for the
Benefit of Agriculture and the Mechanic Arts
New Brunswick, N.J.

*May 9, 1911*

Dear Pennell:

I have not heard from you for many moons, which is probably my fault: but I was led to think of you the other day by seeing the death of poor Ives in the papers.[31] I suppose that was something of a shock to you as it was to me even at this distance. He went pretty quick, which is not a bad way to go if you have to go, but it is a bit startling for one's friend. Almost everyone over here kicks out that way if he isn't killed by a motorcar. Violent deaths in New York seven *per diem*—not inclusive of deaths from canned foods and cold storage. Things are a little "wusser" than when you were here, and each year seems a little closer to the bursting point. We are going to have a scrap here (politically) before long or else all signs fail. I'm getting out of this June 3rd on the "Baltic" and expect to stay out for eight months and come back perhaps with a clearer vision. Shall go to Broadway (England) for a day or so and come down to London about the 12th of June. You might put me up at that swell club of yours if you don't think it too rich for my blood. I won't be in London more than a week. Want to get out before the blooming coronation.[32] Shall go over to Paris and expect to join the McClellans for several weeks, Venice the middle of August; and sailing for Trieste Sept. 16 on Str. "Bohemia" for Bombay. Pack your colors and come along. We may see something worth while. George Peet, a New York lawyer, is going with me. Or if you don't like that then let's go to St. Petersburg in July. What do you say? You have got to go to Italy anyhow to see the show at Venice and Rome. Regards to the "Missous" and yourself.

Yours ever,
Van Dyke

• • •

31. Director of the St. Louis Museum of Art, Halsey Cooley Ives (1847–1911) died in London on May 6, 1911, after suffering an "apoplectic stroke."

32. George V (1865–1936) took the throne in 1910. Van Dyke is referring to the yearlong celebration following the coronation. Among other wonders from around the Empire, attractions featured a pagan temple, a reconstruction of Niagara Falls, and "millions of coloured electric lights in entirely new and matchless designs" ("Coronation Exhibition," *Times* [London], May 1, 1991, 7).

THE LYGON ARMS
Quarters of the Royal Automobile Club
Head Quarters of North Cotswold Hunt
Dates from 1540
Telephone: No. 5
Broadway, Worcestershire

*Thursday, 1911*

Dear Pennell:

I have word from the Grand Hotel that I can't have a bed in the kitchen even; and that they are very sorry. I suppose every tavern keeper in London is consumed with the same kind of sorrow and that if I want a place in London I'll have to rustle for it.

In consequence my plans are somewhat upset. It strikes me just now that there was or used to be some sort of a decent looking tavern or small hotel in a little square just before one gets to your place. It is between your place and The Strand. Perhaps that has escaped the notice of the American contingent and the Colonial phalanx. Would you mind stopping in there and asking if they have one single room for a "single gent"? Anything that is decent at about ten shillings a day would answer. I would take it from Sunday night, or Saturday if necessary, for a week at least. Sunday is such a rotten day in London I would rather not come in until the evening. And will you telegraph me here at my expense or write as you please? If you don't think you are in the room and lodging brokerage business why don't bother.

Hastily,
Van Dyke

[added:] My plans for a "cure" are off. Instead of Harrogate alone I may take Homburg with the McClellans.

RUTGERS COLLEGE
and the
STATE UNIVERSITY OF NEW JERSEY
New Brunswick, New Jersey
Department of Fine Arts

*December 8, 1923*

Dear Pennell:

You haven't reached my state of composure regarding the newspapers.[33] It makes no difference what they say or leave unsaid. Of course, their stupendous ignorance is increasingly amazing as the years go on; but then that is true of all the world. But then *we*, who are assured of immortality, need not worry. Those old Egyptian pharaohs who sat tight with their hands on their knees and a smile on their faces had the right pose.[34]

I'm much pleased to be a member of the "small" (and most exclusive) body on earth. And I recognize that I wouldn't be there were it not for you. Many thanks to you.

Yours ever,
John C. Van Dyke

• • •

33. A reference to the storm of reviews condemning Van Dyke's *Rembrandt and His School* (1923). Through a study of brush strokes and other techniques, the book greatly reduced the number of paintings attributable to the Master. The treatise outraged many critics and collectors, who suffered wounds both to their egos and to their pocketbooks. Though the controversial study made Van Dyke a pioneer in twentieth-century Rembrandt scholarship, at the time he received mostly grief from the official art circles. For more on the long Rembrandt controversy and Van Dyke's place in it, see Bailey.

34. A relative who was a boy at the time remembers the aging but dignified Van Dyke coming over to his house on visits and assuming a similar pose, sitting up straight in a chair with both hands on the head of his cane (Wild, "Interviews and Notes").

RUTGERS COLLEGE
and the
STATE UNIVERSITY OF NEW JERSEY
New Brunswick, New Jersey

*May 1, 1924*

Dear Pennell:

I have been arranging the R. etchings in groups for some time, but the whole bunch of them has been so lied about, forged, copied, and reworked that it is an awful mess to deal with—worse than the paintings.[35] The reworking is the most confusing. It is like repainting a picture, only worse. The Hundred Gilder piece is an illustration. Three or four hands have been at it. Some of the etchings have as many as thirteen states—a "state" meaning only too often that a Jew dealer has bought the plate and has had something put in or ground out by some contemporary genius. The Three Crosses is a holy show and The Three Trees is all balled up in the foreground. Some of the small figures and landscapes are clean enough, and I shall be able to do something with them.

No faith whatever is to be placed in the signature or dates. It was only a trademark of the shop, and anyone used it who needed it in his business. I never knew Chase's opinion of R. or anyone else's, but oddly enough that is the view I have been forced to take of him. The genius was himself but probably lazy, dissolute, and careless. The man who ran the shop and did the work and sold the goods was Van der Pluym.[36] He came from Leyden, was a relative of R., and the guardian of R.'s son Titus. I have a good line on him both in the paintings and the etchings because he was a mannered little cuss. He did the Three Crosses, the Entombment, the Adoration, and many of small-figured huddled groups. But there are many fingers in the R. pie, and no one will do other than curse at us for pointing them out. However, I'll fuss along with it some more. And with the drawings also. When I get some of my dates in shape, I'll come over and show it to you.

Yours ever,
John C. Van Dyke

• • •

35. Van Dyke was working on *The Rembrandt Drawings and Etchings* (1927), a companion volume to *Rembrandt and His School.*

36. For more on Carel Van der Pluym (1630–1672), see Van Dyke, *The Rembrandt Drawings and Etchings* 116–23.

RUTGERS COLLEGE
and the
STATE UNIVERSITY OF NEW JERSEY
New Brunswick, New Jersey

*May 5, 1924*

Dear Pennell:

That is precisely what I have been doing for many months, off and on—comparing for similarity of style. I have a huge magnifying glass about 8 inches in diameter, and I work with that. I have many groups together that I keep sifting and sifting. When I get eight or ten etchings in a group and am certain that one man did them, I then have a long run to determine who the man [is]. When I ever get a style definitely established, I can trust my eye to pick it up wherever and under whatever name I see it; but I have to confirm the style by every scrap of external evidence I can get. I mean, for instance, that when I ever get an idea that Maes did those etchings of the young man model with a clout, I then have to chase the drawing, styles, and all that, through his paintings, sketches, etc.[37]

Of course, you are right, Whistler was right, about a man developing his style but not changing it; but that is the very thing my critics are pounding me about. Fry, Cortissoz, Hofstede de Groot, Valentiner say that I don't take into account the genius of Rembrandt, and Hofstede de Groot goes so far as to say that "no style was foreign to the Great Master."[38] It was the constant irritation of seeing forty different styles in the Rembrandt *oeuvre* that finally drove me to writing that book. There are, for example, 64 portraits of Rembrandt, supposed to be done by himself, seen in 64 different ways, and painted in 64 different ways. The whole thing is absurd.

But I shall worry along with it during the summer and eventually get up something that I shall submit to you.

Hastily,
John C. Van Dyke

· · ·

37. Dutch painter Nicolaes Maes (1634–1693) entered Rembrandt's studio around 1648.

38. Of the art figures in this sentence, Fry likely is Roger Eliot Fry (1866–1934), British painter and critic. More readily identifiable are American art critic Royal Cortissoz (1869–1948), Dutch art historian Cornelis Hofstede de Groot (1863–1930), and German art historian Wilhelm Reinhold Valentiner (1880–1958).

RUTGERS COLLEGE
and the
STATE UNIVERSITY OF NEW JERSEY
New Brunswick, New Jersey

*May 13, 1925*

Dear Pennell:

There was a meeting of the National Institute Council last Friday at which your letter was read, and your suggestion adopted about sending out ballots. You have probably been notified to that effect.

Your further suggestion about the election of officers I will bring up at our next meeting. I quite agree with you that notice of election and names of candidates should be posted or sent to the members of the Institute before the annual meeting. The whole management of the Institute has been more or less informal heretofore, but I have been trying to put it on a more substantial common sense basis.

Things are not what they seem in institutes and academies, nor elsewhere. The world is full of false alarms, and I do not believe things are much more "rotten" here than in England, France, or Germany, or elsewhere. Strange people and strange propositions pop up everywhere and have to be fought off. Which reminds me that you and Hassam[39] had a chance to fight off Brush[40] the other day, but you did not do it, you just sat back and let me do it. You don't believe in the Academy being committed to the Gérôme School of Art any more than I do.[41]

And I do not believe in condemning modern movements. In the Academy it would be accounted to us as academic intolerance rather than esthetic righteousness.[42]

When I looked for you the other day, after getting through with Matthews, you had flown, and I was sorry.[43]

Best regards to Mrs. Pennell.

Yours ever,
John C. Van Dyke

• • •

39. American impressionist Childe Hassam (1859–1935).

40. This possibly is the American artist George de Forest Brush (1855–1941).

41. The fashionable precision of French artist Jean Léon Gérôme (1824–1904) lost its appeal when spontaneity became the watchword of the 1880s. Isolated by change, Gérôme and his tirades against the avant-garde had little effect.

42. Van Dyke is being politic rather than intellectually generous. Five years earlier in *American Painting*, he damned the new art of his day as "gimcrack" and lamented that "all painting seems [to be] going to the dogs with new and incomprehensible conventions" (268).

43. Van Dyke's lifelong friend James Brander Matthews (1852–1929) taught English and dramatic literature at Columbia University and served as president of the Modern Language Association.

QUEENS PARK HOTEL
Port of Spain
Trinidad, B.W.I.

*April 11, 1926*

Dear Pennell:

I have been reading your Scammon Lectures—they have a copy here in the Public Library—and it is excellently done.[44] Just the sort of way to present the subject. It must have had some decided influence on your student auditors. Of course, I agree with almost everything you say—even about Rembrandt. Whistler knew the etching possibilities and facilities better than Rembrandt and did things (the Annie Haden full-length for instance) that Rembrandt never dreamed of.[45] But in what Rembrandt undertook he came off supremely well. I hope to show this in my second Rembrandt book which is ready for the press and I am waiting only to get some further illustrations. I see your Adventures with Writers is advertised but I have not seen the book. I suppose you have sent us all to the devil, which makes for reading.[46]

I'm here in Trinidad waiting for a steamer home. The "Van Dyck" is coming on the 27th and I hope to board her. Will be glad to get back. South America not very interesting for the likes of you and me. It's a little raw with the exception of Rio, which has possibilities. I like the West Indies better, especially Trinidad, which has the best climate of them all, the best hotel, and the most "niggers." I like the "niggers." They are infinitely more poetic than the whites and have towns more picturesque. If you are looking for a health resort and a place to recuperate outside of the world, then come here. Living cheap. Clothing cheap. Dying cheap. I saw a funeral—coffin and hearse advertised at $6.00.[47]

No news from anyone in the U.S. since I left. [Garusey] was with me in Rio for a month. No newspapers. No nothing. None of these island people or those in S.A. know anything about the outside world. The whole U.S. might blow up and they wouldn't hear about it for six months—wouldn't care a cuss even then. Pennell, Member of the American Academy. Scammon lecturer, author of Adventures of an Illustrator, etc., etc.! Why bless your soul they never heard of you nor any of your books or academies! Gott! What a wonderful thing is insularity!

Regards to Mrs. Pennell and yourself. I often think of you both and the old London nights.

Yours ever,
John C. Van Dyke

• • •

44. Pennell's *The Graphic Arts.*

45. Enchanted by his niece Annie Haden, Whistler used her as a subject several times. Likely candidates for Van Dyke's reference are two etchings, *Annie* (1857–1858) and the more dramatic *Annie Haden* (1860) (Lochman plates #24, #137).

46. Mentioned again two paragraphs hence, the correct title is *The Adventures of an Illustrator.* Pennell praises Van Dyke twice. As to writers on art, "there are no authoritative critics in America, save John Van Dyke" (260). Pennell also cites Van Dyke as the "delightful person" with whom he did *The New New York* (316).

47. For more on Van Dyke's contrasting estimate of South America and the West Indies, see his autobiography (184–91). His *In the West Indies* rhapsodizes:

> Chemistry cannot turn out bright enough colors, nor dictionaries sufficient winged words to tell the splendor of these islands. The glory of their light, the rose and violet of their atmosphere, the high key of their color cannot be exaggerated. Pictorially, they are intangible dreams, fantasies that the retina records confusedly, and the hand grasps feebly. (vii)

The quote supports one witty critic's comment that Art for Art's Sake was about nothing more than stimulation of the optic nerve.

## SMITHSONIAN INSTITUTION
## *Archives of American Art, Carnegie Institute**

### CARNEGIE INSTITUTE

*[undated fragment; 1895]*

Mr. Weidner, too, has excellent pictures including Manet's "Toreador Dead," one of the best pieces of painting in all the

* Courtesy of the Archives of American Art, Smithsonian Institution.

world. If you write these men and say what the New York men are willing to do, I am sure they would co-operate. In Cleveland Mr. Pope has three Whistlers that Mr. Inglis could get for you.

So soon as I hear from you about your plan I will communicate with Inglis, Ellsworth, and Fuller. I don't know how it is that I have been dragged into this matter, but I am interested in it and will do what I can to make a success of it.[48]

Yours very truly,
John C. Van Dyke

• • •

48. In the summer of 1895, Van Dyke scrambled to assemble contemporary paintings for an exhibition at the Carnegie Institute. This was a new cultural complex funded by Carnegie and scheduled to open in the fall of that year. Together with other correspondence at the Smithsonian, this fragment of a letter shows Van Dyke at the very center of the art world. He wrote to the nation's most powerful art collectors, whose wealth was the engine for "culture" at the time, requesting loans of their famous works. Carnegie, not beyond a windy pride at the grand opening, must have been pleased at his young art adviser's success. The Smithsonian letters show Van Dyke gathering paintings by Monet, Manet, Whistler, Ryder—a whole host of the great art of the period. This work for Carnegie is a dramatic illustration of the aesthetic values Van Dyke would soon impose upon the desert.

## NEW YORK PUBLIC LIBRARY
## *Century Magazine Collection**

RUTGERS COLLEGE
New Brunswick, N.J.

*April 2, 1892*

Dear Mr. Gilder:[49]

Thank you for your letter of the 30th ult. I shall endeavor to get up the brief paper you desire upon the Lotto Colum-

* Century Company Records, Rare Books and Manuscripts Division, the New York Public Library, Astor, Lenox and Tilden Foundations.

bus. Anything on Columbus at this time would of necessity be brief. I thought, however, that this picture was of sufficient importance to call for something more than a half page, especially now. Hence, my note to Mr. Drake.

I shall get up the paper concisely, and you shall judge of its probable interest to the public.[50]

Yours very truly,
John C. Van Dyke

• • •

49. Richard Watson Gilder (1844–1909), poet and public-spirited citizen, served as the editor of the influential *Century Magazine* from 1881 until his death.

50. As Van Dyke explains in his autobiography, the issue in this letter concerns a hot dispute over a painting Van Dyke discovered in Venice. Judging it to be by Italian artist Lorenzo Lotto, Van Dyke touted the canvas as the only authentic portrait of Christopher Columbus. After Van Dyke pulled strings with his wealthy art aficionados, the canvas was given prominent display at the Chicago World's Fair of 1893, commemorating the four-hundredth anniversary of Columbus's discovery, and it was reproduced on the tickets, medals, and other bric-a-brac of the fair. However, many critics challenged Van Dyke's assessments that the portrait was of Columbus and that Lotto had painted it (83). Van Dyke presented his side of the argument in "The Lotto Portrait of Columbus," which appeared in *Century Magazine*. With the passage of the years, Van Dyke's certitude on the matter began to waver. See his letter of June 6, 1904, to August F. Jaccaci, in the next section.

THEOLOGICAL SEMINARY
New Brunswick
New Jersey

*October 9, 1893*

My Dear Mr. Gilder:

I return the paper on "Painting at the Fair" with such changes as you suggested and with such "cutting" as it would bear.

I cannot think the original statements were too strong for truth, but you are probably right in thinking as much effect could be had by milder statements. I put it strongly purposely to make the article readable and because I wanted to say a spade was a spade without circumlocution. However, I don't question the wisdom of your suggestions. You are the better judge.

If it needs further toning down, say where and send it back to me, please.

I thank you for a hundred dollar check.

Yours very truly,
John C. Van Dyke

[added as P.S.:]

The Scandinavian painting. I am not disposed to believe the latest praise of Paris as some of our Paris fellows seem to think. The French certainly did not think so in 1889, and the work itself is a direct disclaimer of such an idea. They got something of technic from Paris, but at bottom they are themselves, just as many of our Americans are—only more so. It is the art fashion nowadays to attribute everything to Paris, but it is not always the truth.

R. W. Gilder, Esq.
Century Magazine

THEOLOGICAL SEMINARY
New Brunswick
New Jersey

*May 1, 1894*

Dear Mr. Gilder:

I have cut and slashed and prayed and sworn over this article all the morning. There is nearly a page knocked out, and I don't see how more could be eliminated without wrecking it entirely. It limps now like a blind beggar.

Some things I have cut out positively and some with a "?" You decide about these latter.

Yours very truly,
John C. Van Dyke

RUTGERS COLLEGE
and
RUTGERS SCIENTIFIC SCHOOL
The New Jersey State College for the
Benefit of Agriculture and the Mechanic Arts
New Brunswick, N.J.

*January 23, 1896*

Dear Mr. Johnson:[51]

I will go up to Barnard's studio Sunday afternoon and see the "Pan" and make some report to you as to how it will pan out.

It will hardly do to "discover" Barnard in the magazine. I saw half a dozen of his things in the Champ-de-Mars Salon of 1894, and if I am not "off" there was a big showing of his things at the old Salon that year that attracted some attention. If it is the man I mean, he is a follower of Rodin and a believer in the suggestiveness of the incomplete *idea.* Michael Angelo and Rodin. But I will see and let you know.

Yours very truly,
John C. Van Dyke

• • •

51. Beginning in 1881 poet and civic leader Robert Underwood Johnson (1853–1937) served as associate editor of *Century Magazine.* Upon Gilder's death in 1909, Johnson took over the editorship.

RUTGERS COLLEGE
and
RUTGERS SCIENTIFIC SCHOOL
The New Jersey State College for the
Benefit of Agriculture and the Mechanic Arts
New Brunswick, N.J.

*February 27, 1896*

Dear Johnson:

The "Bucking Broncho" [*sic*] is familiar Knowledge with me, not only in Remington's bronze but in the real life, but I don't see how I can write about it. I can't treat the bronze as great art, and I don't care to write about it as history. Let me off from that, please, and let me suggest Theodore Roosevelt as the man who could give you half a page of more interesting reading on the subject than could I.

Thank you very much for asking me to write it, and don't take my declination amiss.[52]

Yours faithfully,
John C. Van Dyke

• • •

52. Though Van Dyke did not always hew to his own pronouncements, in the main he detested realism in art as lowbrow and "contemptible" (*Principles of Art* 176). His commitment to "high" art excluded such popular subjects as the cowboys and bucking horses favored by Frederic Remington and other Western artists then coming into vogue. Of the bronze in question, Ballinger states: "Remington's first bronze, *Bronco Buster* [1895] . . . was based on the many photographs, experiences, and previous works he had produced, mostly from ranches in Texas and Sonora. . . . [H]is action packed sculpture was to become an icon of American art and the West" (66). For a photo of the sculpture, see 68.

Van Dyke's autobiography hints at nettles in the relationship between Van Dyke and Theodore Roosevelt (60). By suggesting that Roosevelt write the piece, Van Dyke is implying a put-down. At any rate, robust outdoorsman and politician Theodore Roosevelt, an admirer of Remington, did not write on the *Bronco Buster* for *Century*.

THE FIRST AVENUE HOTEL
High Holborn
London

*July 19, 1896*

Dear Mr. Gilder:

Since my arrival here I have had several talks with Mr. Cole and have been out with him two afternoons looking at "Old English Masters."[53] We are in perfect accord and will have no trouble in working together. I shall be sadly out of my reckoning if we do not get up an interesting series of pictures, though the lack of good figure pieces and the predominance of portraits bothers me a little. I shall not, however, make up the complete list until I have seen all the pictures in England and Scotland. Yesterday I was hunting through Guildhall and the Drapers Guild, and tomorrow I go to Windsor.

The series cannot be started in the November number. Mr. Cole has only two Hogarths ready, and we want four blocks. He is now working on Gainsborough's "Mrs. Siddons," while we are deciding about the two additional Hogarths. The two already done are the "Shrimp Girl" and portrait of Hogarth at his easel, in the Portrait Gallery. This latter is a beautiful little work, and Hogarth is a very important man. The English have cackled over him as a satirist, but not a single writer has half understood him *as a painter.* I shall have something new to say on that score.

We want one complete satirical piece by Hogarth, and at present writing I am favorably inclined to the [illegible word]. The "Rake's Progress" and "Marriage à la Mode" are all too small, too huddled, and too "detailed" to make good blocks. The charming bits in these would be lost in the engraving. For a fourth engraving I want a good "detail" thrown up large on the block, and nothing could be finer from a point of art than the figure of the woman pulling off her stockings in the "Orgies" (Rake's Progress.) I am, however, afraid of the subject for the magazine. (If you do not remember it you can refresh your memory from the folio of plates at The Players). Cole says we could get the upper half of this figure very well, but that would lose the *abandon* of the whole figure. Do you think we had better try it at all? It is the loveliest piece of painting Hogarth ever did.

Romney's "Parson's Daughter" is a round picture and will have to be reduced for the Century page and even then will look awkward. The picture could be made a square upright and would gain immensely in the engraving. Will you ask Mr. Drake what he thinks of taking that liberty with the picture? I should, of course, explain the matter in the text. Mr. Cole agrees with me, but neither of us cares to go ahead without consultation with the home office.

At the present time, I do not see how we can have more than fifteen painters without striking pretty poor timber. Nor will there be more than about forty-five blocks—the half dozen big men. Hogarth, Reynolds, Gainsborough, Lawrence, and Turner receiving four each. The painters will be taken up chronologically by Mr. Cole, with the exception of Wilson, who comes second in point of time, but I shall place him fourth in the magazine.

I want to make an impression at the start by having Reynolds and Gainsborough follow Hogarth.

Yours very truly,
John C. Van Dye
c/o Brown Shipley & Co, London

· · ·

53. This series, with text by Van Dyke and engravings by Timothy Cole, appeared in *Century* from 1897 through 1899. The Century Company later issued the series as a book with the same title. With the perceptive grace of his prose, Van Dyke explicates the Masters. Covering the period from about 1750 to 1850, the book includes such figures as William Hogarth, Sir Joshua Reynolds, Thomas Gainsborough, J. M. W. Turner, and John Constable. The volume also shows the sharp and studied way of seeing Van Dyke would soon apply to the "canvases" of desert landscapes.

THE FIRST AVENUE HOTEL
High Holborn
London

*August 14, 1896*

My Dear Mr. Gilder:

I have your letter about the Romney "Parson's Daughter." Since writing you, I have re-examined the picture. The canvas is *square.* There is no sign of an oval upon it and never was at any time. The oval impression is altogether in the framing. There is an oval gold mat inside of the square frame. I don't suppose it will be necessary to *engrave the frame!* The picture if squared up will come out larger and better in every way, showing the free handling and the expression to advantage. An oval or round picture will not fill space on the block decoratively and will require a reduction in the size of the head and faces. However, I will be home before Cole gets started on Romney, and we can settle the matter there.

I wrote Mr. Chichester about a plan I was working upon to get Sir Chas. [illegible name] consent to the engraving of some of his pictures. Please say to Mr. Chichester that the plan succeeded. Sir Chas. consents to the engraving, and we thereby get one of the most fetching pictures by Reynolds in England, also two Constables, a Romney, and a Hoppner—all of the finest quality.

I hope to have the whole list completed before leaving, and I think when you see it that you will agree with me in thinking it attractive.

The Hogarth "Stocking" picture has been abandoned. We shall do a detail from the "Marriage à la Mode" instead—a delicate bit of satire from the "Marriage Contract." While deciding about the Hogarth, Mr. Cole has done the "Mrs. Siddons" by Gainsborough. It is very lovely. Whistler is quite enchanted with the block.

I am off tomorrow morning for Norwich and the north. I have letters to all the officials at Glasglow and Edinborough and shall have little trouble in getting what I want there. I'm also going to the Duke of Devonshire's place and Earl Spencer's. The former consents to the engraving of the charming "Duchess of Devonshire & Child" by Reynolds and has sent me word to come to his place when I choose and that Mr. Cole is to have free access.

It won't hurt this series any to have lordly subjects or rather grand lady subjects, the pictures hailing from lordly collections. We will have three or four things from the Queen to begin with, and Lord Carlisle, with a peppering of Dukes and Earls, won't cause people to "stop the magazine."

Yours very truly,
John C. Van Dyke

R. W. Gilden, Esq.

*Lock Box 821*
*Los Angeles, Cal.*
*September 6 [1899]*[54]

Dear Mr. Gilder:

Your letter of enquiry about my address has been sent to me here. The permanent address is as above, or New Brunswick, though I shall shortly be going to Mexico. It has been quite recently decided that I stay West or South this winter. I have a small patch of localized bronchitis in the left lung, upper part. To go back to a New York winter with it simply means more trouble. Now that I am out here, I may as well make a good job of it. The doctors say "not serious" and that I will get rid of it all right.

Can you write me what you wish me to do? Evidently you

are preparing to "cut" some of the Old English Masters articles by removing some of the articles and engravings. All right. Anything you say. I have my materials with me and shall finish all the articles before Christmas. Ask Mr. Chichester when he wishes to bring out the book. If for Christmas 1900, I can easily get it ready for the printer by May 1st. Ask Mr. Chichester to write me about it.[55]

Yours very truly,
John C. Van Dyke

R. W. Gilder, Esq.
The Century Magazine
New York

• • •

54. Though Van Dyke did not include the year of this letter, someone wrote "1899" to the left of the address. This likely is correct. Using the same address, Van Dyke wrote another letter, not reproduced, to Gilder on October 28, 1899. The year fits with the sequence of the two following letters, written from Mexico. All three letters lend further support to the probability that Van Dyke first traveled to the Southwest in 1899, not 1898, as earlier supposed. See Van Dyke, *Autobiography* 117, 234–37 n. 1.

55. The book, *Old English Masters*, did not appear until 1902.

HOTEL ALMADA[56]
Antiguo Cosmopolita
M. Marchebout, Propietario
Calle de Muelle
Hotel Moderno de Primera Clase
Guaymas[57]

*December 3, 1899*

Dear Carey:

The Lawrence "Lady Derby" belongs to Lord de Grey Wilton. The name on the list is correct. It is not Lord *Grey de* Wilton. I thought that must be the name, but when in England I looked him up in the Peerage book.

Mexico very beautiful. Climate here superb, beating California all to pieces. Just the same, I would like mighty well to be back in New York. When a man is in exile he can't help hankering after home and friends. But I'm progressing favorably and may yet live to torment the public with more art books. Regards to you.

Yours very truly,
John C. Van Dyke

[added at bottom:] Make a "Memo" of my address for the winter. c/o Hotel Almada. Guaymas, Sonora, Mexico.

[added in the margin, to the left of Van Dyke's signature:] Good! R.W.G.

• • •

56. Typical of Van Dyke on his travels, he was staying in one of the best hotels available, this one owned by the politically powerful Almada family.

57. The Mexican city of Guaymas, in the state of Sonora, is about 230 miles south of the international border. Backed by the desert, facing the Gulf of California, it has warm and sparkling winters.

HOTEL ALMADA
Antiguo Cosmopolita
M. Marchebout, Propietario
Calle de Muelle
Hotel Moderno de Primera Clase
Guaymas

*April 1, 1901*

Dear Mr. Gilder:

I have your letter about the "American Painters" Series.[58] I don't know exactly the status of the series but think I wrote two or three articles and perhaps left the first one with you. I shall be home in June, and perhaps you can let the matter rest until then. But if it's urgent, why, go ahead and ask Hart to do them. I promise to have no heart-burnings about it. In fact, I might feel relieved, for just now my spirits are down so low that I couldn't write anything but a dirge. I've just finished a book on "The Desert" that is full of arid howls. Two years in the sands with Mexicans and rattlesnakes for Company do not develop cheerfulness.

Mexican winter climate, *west of the Sierras*, is the finest on this

Continent, but Mexican life is simply "God-awful," as they say in Arizona.

Yours very truly,
John C. Van Dyke

R. W. Gilder, Esq.

• • •

58. Though Van Dyke published many articles on American artists for several magazines, he wrote no such series for *Century* under this title.

RUTGERS COLLEGE
New Brunswick, New Jersey

*April 18, 1910*

My Dear Johnson:

I have your note, also that "Short article" which you kindly ask about; but it isn't the kind of article you want. I am going to the Rockies in a couple of months, and to India and the Himalayas in January, and I may scare up something for you there.

But in the meantime I shall see you.

Yours very truly,
John C. Van Dyke

R. U. Johnson, Esq.
Editor, Century Magazine
New York

[typewritten]

RUTGERS COLLEGE
New Brunswick, New Jersey

*April 20, 1910*

Mr. R. U. Johnson
Editor of the Century magazine
New York, N.Y.

Dear Johnson:

About the only Rembrandt portrait of himself that I know of in America belongs to Henry C. Frick, Fiftieth Street and Fifth

Avenue.[59] It is a large and a very important picture, one of the best in the country beyond doubt. I do not remember if it has been engraved. No doubt Mr. Frick would be quite willing to let you reproduce it. The picture called "The Noble Slav" by Rembrandt, belonging to William K. Vanderbilt, is of course a fine example of Rembrandt also.

Yours, truly,
John C. Van Dyke

· · ·

59. Industrialist Henry Clay Frick (1849–1919) willed his mansion and art collection to New York City. He was first an ally, then an enemy, of Van Dyke's friend Andrew Carnegie.

[typewritten]

RUTGERS COLLEGE
New Brunswick, New Jersey

*November 4, 1910*

Mr. Robert Underwood Johnson
Editor, Century Magazine
33 E. 17th St.
New York

My Dear Mr. Johnson:

I enclose you the note about Lincoln, which you asked for. The only question is as to whether the incident is of sufficient interest to publish. If it is, use it. If it isn't, I shan't be grieved about throwing it in the waste-paper basket.[60]

Yours very truly,
John C. Van Dyke

[In manuscript, the letter is followed by a plain sheet of paper with various jottings. Most significant is "This Poe incident seems significant, doesn't it? R.U.J."]

· · ·

60. The piece appeared as "Lincoln's Reading and Modesty." Drawing on a family anecdote, Van Dyke illustrates that, contrary to the myth, Lin-

coln had good access to reading material on the frontier, was well-read, and appreciated the work of Edgar Allan Poe. Also illustrating Lincoln's modesty, Van Dyke recounts two stories about the relationship of Lincoln and Van Dyke's father in Congress. However, the account maintains its own modesty by not naming the father. It is a typical Van Dyke touch.

Years later Van Dyke included the stories in his autobiography (12–14).

## SMITHSONIAN INSTITUTION
## *Archives of American Art, August F. Jaccaci Papers**

RUTGERS COLLEGE
and
RUTGERS SCIENTIFIC SCHOOL
The New Jersey State College for the
Benefit of Agriculture and the Mechanic Arts
New Brunswick, N.J.

*June 6, 1904*

My Dear Mr. Jacacci [*sic*]:[61]

Thank you for the check, which came in this morning and which I shall find use for this summer. I enclose a receipt.

My recollection about the Columbus portrait corresponds with Mr. Ellsworth's. Capt. Mason and I saw it first in Venice in the house of Arturio della Ronce. He was interested in it as a possible Columbus for the World Fair in Chicago (the year was 1892, I think), and I looked at it more as a possible Lotto. Stillman had seen it and pronounced it both Lotto and Columbus. The picture is not [illegible word] positive proof for either one or the other now. It is certainly *Lottoesque*, but the repainting interferes with minute examination. As for Columbus and his "only one portrait," that never will be settled. I believe this portrait is as likely as any and really more probable than any other in existence.

---

* Courtesy of the Archives of American Art, Smithsonian Institution.

Perhaps I can see you Friday at the lunch or at Museum or the Century.

Yours very truly,
John C. Van Dyke

A. F. Jacacci [*sic*], Esq.
452 Fifth Avenue
New York

• • •

61. Born in France, mural painter and writer Augusto Floriano Jaccaci (1856–1930) came to the United States in the 1880s to edit a multivolume reference work on American painting with American painter and art critic John La Farge. After a slow start, the project fell through with La Farge's death in 1910.

RUTGERS COLLEGE
and
RUTGERS SCIENTIFIC SCHOOL
The New Jersey State College for the
Benefit of Agriculture and the Mechanic Arts
New Brunswick, N.J.

*October* 10 *[no year]*

Dear Jacacci [*sic*]:

I left at the office of the Century Club for you that package of papers about the "Afterglow" by Inness and also my alleged "article" on the picture—for which I won't apologize. You didn't give me anything to write about, and besides Cox had already written it and anyway I hadn't a brain in my head about the thing.

This was on Saturday afternoon. I had expected to see you and deliver "the goods" personally, but you did not show up. Sorry you didn't, for we had a pleasant evening.

Yours ever,
John C. Van Dyke

## BARSTOW PRINTER REVIEW

*The following selections are not John C. Van Dyke's correspondence. Rather, the editors have taken excerpts regarding Van Dyke from the reminiscences of his nephew, Dix, as published in the* Barstow Printer Review *in the fall of 1953.*

[Thursday, September 17, 1953]

John Muir, the famous naturalist, brought his daughter Helen to [Theodore Van Dyke's] ranch to remain for her health. [The Muirs] were wealthy, and Muir decided to build her a dwelling house. He was Scotch and had in his youth endured extreme poverty. Though naturally a generous soul, he now displayed extreme penuriousness. It resulted in a tiny shack with one room and a porch. He made a bunk two-feet wide for the nurse and was much provoked when that lady insisted on it being wider. "These damn Dutch are all used to big beds of feather ticks," he lamented.

Miss Muir imported a saddle horse and shocked the village grannies, both male and female, by riding astride with a divided skirt. It resulted in some acrimonious debates in which Dix joined. He hated side saddles because they caused sores on horses. . . .

In June the rabbits became very numerous. They dug under the fence and finally learned to make holes in the wire. Shooting them produced results until the rabbits learned to invade the alfalfa field after dark and leave before morning. Efforts to plug the holes were futile. Mr. Funk conceived the idea of having Buel patrol the fence all night with a lantern and close the holes.[62]

The next morning the field was full of rabbits running about and seeking a hole. None seemed to know how to make a hole to escape. Buel reported that during the night he had seen droves of them. He continued his patrol for two weeks. Each morning at daylight all hands, on foot, horseback, and with dogs, herded the rabbits into pens and clubbed them to death. It may have been sport for some but not when it was followed by ten hours of arduous labor in the hayfield. When the rabbits were being beaten to death with clubs, many cried in piercing shrieks, like a tortured child. It was a rather sickening job and so disgusted Dix that several years elapsed before he could eat a jack rabbit.

John Muir had made many and long solitary journeys among the Sierra Nevada Mountains, equipped with a bag of bread and some tea. He would never catch a fish or kill any bird or animal. He would eat them when someone else prepared and cooked them. He had been a hunter in his youth but had developed an aversion to taking life. One morning he was enticed out to see the rabbits corralled. He was very much interested until they were penned and the slaughter began. Then in great disgust he retreated to the house. "That was a very brutal exhibition," he declared. . . .

The Judge's brother came from New Jersey for a visit. He was a scholarly, dignified gentleman who taught book larnin' in a college and wrote books on art and nature and various highbrowed subjects. He looked soft and grumbled about ill health but thought nothing of roaming about the desert on the hottest summer day for eight hours without a drink or anything to eat. He tried to demonstrate that he could keep out rabbits by closing their holes. The rabbits were not deterred, but he derived some gratification from clubbing some.

[From Thursday, October 29, 1953]

The Judge was getting old, but his health remained good. He no longer wrote for publication but continued to paint pictures and daily pored over his beloved tomes of ancient Greek and Latin. Occasionally he toiled in his small vegetable garden or walked to the village where he drank beer and conversed with the few old men who doddered about. They respected his learning and regarded him with esteem, but they were not his kind, and he hungered for intellectual companionship.

He was ever delighted when Muir paid an occasional visit to the ranch. He had enjoyed Muir's visits to the ranch, when the two spent much of their time together. They found each other congenial souls and never disagreed on any topic.

Not so the Judge's brother. He came during one of Muir's visits, and the two wrangled incessantly about various highbrow subjects. Muir came no more, and the brother's visits were far apart.[63]

• • •

62. In a few years, Helen Muir married Buel, the son of ranch partner Hugh Funk. Building a large mansion called Desertaire near the Van Dyke Ranch, the couple continued to live in the Daggett area.

63. In contrast to the unpleasantness Dix describes here, name-dropping John C. Van Dyke includes in his autobiography a breezy version of his meeting with John Muir (167–68). In fact, records Van Dyke of his encounter with the famed writer and conservationist, "I was . . . much flattered by his saying in his simple Scotch way that he had made this trip, at this time, that he might meet me" (167).

## SOUTHWEST MUSEUM
## *Charles F. Lummis Manuscript Collection**

### Thursday, July 30, 1908 El Alisal[64]

. . . trotted over to Dockweiler's and in five minutes straightened out a book order fuss for some 1,500 volumes which had torn two of our departments and two book firms wide open; and then to the City Hall to hold up the Building Inspector to let me have a private roof garden for the girls of the staff when he wouldn't let Hamburger put up a shelter for a cat.

Then John C. Van Dyke, who wrote a good book about the Desert, came by appointment to the Library and I fotched him home and we had supper and a nice concert—though Amate had skinned out somewhere else.[65] But Nacho and his wife were here and he played beautifully and Maria did herself proud—and the old man accompanied her on the guitar in quite extraordinary fashion—considering. Anyway, Van Dyke enjoyed it and so did we.

Now it's in the thick of work for the Southwest Museum

* Courtesy of the Southwest Museum, Los Angeles, CA. Charles F. Lummis Manuscript Collection, folder #MS1.1.4440.

Directors' meetings and meetings of the Executive Committee of the Southwest Society and a few other little things—and me to the grindstone.

. . .

64. Like the Dix Van Dyke selections, the following excerpt is not John C. Van Dyke's correspondence. Rather, it is passages from the diary of Charles F. Lummis, recording the two men's acquaintance.

65. At the time, Lummis was the head of the Los Angeles Public Library. He later helped found the Southwest Museum, whose archives contain Lummis's annotated copy of Van Dyke's *The Desert.*

[typewritten]

Founder's Day

RUTGERS COLLEGE
and the
STATE UNIVERSITY OF NEW JERSEY
New Brunswick, New Jersey
Department of Fine Arts

*February 12, 1923*

Dr. Charles F. Lummis
Los Angeles, California

Dear Lummis:

I am glad to join in the chorus—the paean of praise unmixed—which is being offered you on your birthday. I don't know why you are having a birthday, because by looking you up in Who's Who I find you are a younger man than myself. But I am glad you are alive and still going strong. Keep it up. No one knows what latent potentialities are still to be found in a man in the sixties. One's vision always gets clearer as he nears the seventies, which is not an altogether unmixed blessing, because he is able to see the many stupidities that he himself has perpetrated in the past. But it gives one perspective and sense of proportion not known to a younger man.

I remember a Spanish dinner at your house many years ago, with wine, women, and song—remember it with much pleasure.

Perhaps I shall see you again, as I am thinking of coming to California soon for a visit. The land of the great Southwest has always been very attractive to me, and it has been a regret of my life that I have not been able to live there. Unfortunately, most of my interests carry me to the East instead of the West, and so runs my world away.

Regards to you, and many years of happy days attend you.

Yours very truly,
John C. Van Dyke

[typewritten]

RUTGERS COLLEGE
and the
STATE UNIVERSITY OF NEW JERSEY
New Brunswick, New Jersey

*Feb. 19, 1924*

Mr. John Comstock
Southwest Museum
Los Angeles, Calif.

My Dear Mr. Comstock:

Thank you very much for your invitation to attend the reception on Founder's Day to be given to Charles F. Lummis. I regret exceedingly that I cannot come—I always regret that I cannot come to California. It is the one place where I should like to live, but at present indications it looks as though I should not even get a chance to die there. One of the joys of living there would be to see Lummis. Will you please tell him so for me, and wish him a long life and a crown of glory?

Yours very truly,
John C. Van Dyke

## AMERICAN ACADEMY OF ARTS AND LETTERS
## *John C. Van Dyke Papers**

RUTGERS COLLEGE
and
RUTGERS SCIENTIFIC SCHOOL
The New Jersey State College for the
Benefit of Agriculture and the Mechanic Arts
New Brunswick, N.J.

*March 3, 1908*

Dear Johnson:[66]

I don't know anything about the National Institute of Arts and Letters but if anyone thinks I can do any good by belonging to it why from [*sic*] consider that I have accepted my election to membership, notice of which you have kindly sent me.

Yours very truly,
John C. Van Dyke

R. W. Johnson, Secy.

• • •

66. At the time associate editor of *Century Magazine*, Robert Underwood Johnson also served as secretary of the American Academy.

[typewritten]

RUTGERS COLLEGE
New Brunswick, New Jersey

*October 25, 1909*

Robert Underwood Johnson
*Century Magazine*

Dear Johnson:

Thank you very much for thinking of me as a possible speaker at the Saint-Gaudens[67] Presentation, but I fear I shall have to

* Courtesy of the American Academy of Arts and Letters, New York City.

forego the pleasure. I have not spoken in public in half a dozen years, because of chronic pharyngitis. For the last four months it has assumed an acute condition and I am now in the doctor's hands having my gullet burned with nitrate of silver every day or so.[68] He would not hear of my making anything like a public address. All of which I regret.

Royal Cortissoz knows the subject and so does Hamilton Morris and I should think either of them would be acceptable for the occasion.

Yours very truly,
John C. Van Dyke

• • •

67. Augustus Saint-Gaudens (1848–1907) was an Irish-born American sculptor educated at the Cooper Institute and the École des Beaux-Arts. He is best known for his Lincoln in Lincoln Park, Chicago, and the Shaw Memorial in Boston.

68. Silver nitrate was used as a caustic, germicide, antiseptic, and astringent. Not understood in Van Dyke's day, its effects could be ferocious, both on the body and the mind.

Silver nitrate was commonly prescribed as a treatment for tuberculosis and for a variety of respiratory conditions, among other things. This latter we know Van Dyke had. In view of this, Van Dyke was unwittingly taking what was essentially a poison, and in view of his chronic respiratory condition, he may have been taking it over the years. In the case of pharyngitis mentioned in the letter, the sore throat was painted with the chemical. The side effects of long use could be many and dangerous, including damage to the liver and kidneys and a variety of intestinal upheavals—not to mention depression over the worsening condition. Unfortunately, when the patient became sicker from the misguided treatment, the response often was to increase the dosage. Such was the faith in silver nitrate. Silver nitrate also could darken the patient's skin (Amdur, Doull, and Klaassen 669). Seizures and dizziness have been reported anecdotally.

The effects on Van Dyke's mental state could have been severe. Silver and other metals have been implicated in causing confusion or dementia (Sullivan and Krieger 156). Many of the symptoms discussed above match Van Dyke's complaints throughout his letters and autobiography.

Furthermore, the darkening of the skin may be involved in a physical description referring to Van Dyke's "olive" skin (Mather 19: 189).

[typed form; addresses filled in by hand]

American Academy of Arts and Letters
633 West 155th Street
New York City

The following are members of my family and friends whom I wish invited to the Academy functions:[69]

Mr. and Mrs. Harry L. Parr
35 Gilbert Place, Yonkers, New York

Mrs. Horace E. Andrews
Saint James, Long Island, New York

The Countess Mercati
1 Sutton Place, New York City

Miss Sarah Cooper Hewitt
9 Lexington Avenue, New York City

Mr. and Mrs. George B. McClellan
2424 California Street, Washington, D.C.

Mrs. Andrew Carnegie
2 East 91st Street, New York

signed: John C. Van Dyke

• • •

69. Some people on the list are readily identifiable:

Mr. and Mrs. Harry L. Parr. Mrs. Parr, Van Dyke's daughter, Clare Van Dyke Parr, was married to Harry L. Parr, a professor of engineering at Columbia University (Strong xi).

The Countess Mercati. A patron of the arts who supported symphonies, operas, and ballet in New York City. She was "the widow of Count Alexander Mercati of the royal court of Greece" ("Countess Mercati, Patron of the Arts").

Mentioned earlier, Mr. and Mrs. George B. McClellan were patrons of the arts and Van Dyke's lifelong friends.

Mrs. Andrew Carnegie was, of course, the wife of steel magnate Andrew Carnegie.

*New Brunswick, N.J.*
*December 6, 1923*

Dear Sir:

I have great pleasure in acknowledging your announcement of my election to a membership in the American Academy of Arts and Letters. The honor of such an election is so unique and distinctive that no one could fail to appreciate it. I am glad to signify to you my acceptance and, with it, my disposition to further the aims of the Academy in any way that may be possible for me.

I have the honor to remain

Yours very truly,
John C. Van Dyke

Mr. Robert Underwood Johnson
Secretary

[typewritten]

RUTGERS COLLEGE
and the
STATE UNIVERSITY OF NEW JERSEY
New Brunswick, New Jersey
Department of Fine Arts

*December 19, 1923*

Mrs. William Vanamee
American Academy of Arts and Letters
633 West 155th Street
New York, N.Y.

Dear Mrs. Vanamee:

The way I generally answer letters such as the enclosed is to throw them into the waste basket. I have received several score of such letters within the last few weeks.[70] It is impossible to answer them, and the people have no business to ask you for such information.

If you answer it at all, the best thing you can say is that the *Bishop of Blois* may be worth $5.00 or $5,000—you cannot tell until you see the picture.

Yours very truly,
John C. Van Dyke

· · ·

70. A flurry of unwelcome letters followed the publication of Van Dyke's *Rembrandt and His School.* The radically revisionist study of the master's oeuvre speared both critics and collectors, and the storm the book caused in the press brought Van Dyke to public notice.

*New Brunswick, New Jersey*
*November 5, 1925*

Mrs. William Vanamee
National Institute of Arts & Letters
633 West 155th Street
New York, New York

My Dear Mrs. Vanamee:

The Council meeting yesterday was attended by only five members. The majority present, Morris, Damrosch, and Finley, voted for a round-robin letter to the Council members asking a vote on recommending to the Institute the names of Mrs. Wharton and Miss Repplier. Van Dyke and Aitken opposed—I on the legality of the proceeding. I served notice that I would fight it all along the line. But it was agreed that the ballot by letter should be taken. So will you send it out to all the members of the Council, asking if they agree or disagree on the recommendation of Miss Wharton [*sic*][71] and Miss Repplier to the Institute? Wait four days for answers. If, at the end of four days, you have six affirmative votes, then the names should be put on the ballot to be voted at the Institute meeting on November 19th. A two-thirds vote of the Council (six votes) is necessary under the Constitution. If there are fewer than six votes you should take no action about the names. There were five votes of Council recorded for the other candidates, and I am writing Mr. Henderson and Mr. Betts today to get the necessary six.

Yours very truly,
John C. Van Dyke

[added in Van Dyke's hand at the bottom and up the right-hand margin:] The minutes were left for you at the office of the Century Club, 7 West 43d Street. Mr. Kendall is in Europe, and I presume it is not worth sending word to him, as his vote could not be received in time. I have written [illegible name], Aitken, Betts, and Henderson, asking them to vote "No" and enclosing a stamped envelope to your address, but that will not render letters to them by you unnecessary.

• • •

71. Edith Wharton had divorced Edward Wharton in 1913.

*New Brunswick, New Jersey*
*November 9, 1925*

My Dear Mrs. Vanamee:

I am in bed with an attack of bronchitis, and my doctor thinks I should not attempt to preside at the Institute dinner on November 19. He wants me to get away south as soon as I can travel.

I have written Dr. Finley and asked him to call a Council Meeting, or arrange by telephone to have a presiding officer appointed from the Vice Presidents—presumably Dr. Damrosch or Mr. Henderson. Will you cooperate with Dr. Finley? I have also said I would ask you to preface an agenda for the presiding officer, and also for the secretary pro tem, who will be Mr. Aitken. In the agenda for the presiding officer you should place, for adoption or rejection, the "Plan for the Enlarged Activities of the Institute." It has been endorsed by the Council and recommended for adoption and has been before the Institute for over a year—the printed plan having been twice mailed to members of the Institute. It now requires merely to be voted upon by the members of the Institute on November 19.

I enclose you a letter from Mr. Henderson regarding the ballot on sending the names of Mrs. Wharton and Miss Repplier up to the Institute. His vote (in the absence of Mr. Kendall) with mine and Mr. Aitken's is sufficient to nullify such action, even if the other five members of the Council vote in the affirmative. It requires six votes to carry.

I hope to heaven they will settle that woman question! I'm weary of it.

Thank you very much for the great help you have been to all of us in keeping us going on a straight road. And will you lend a helping hand to the pro-tem presiding officer, who may be a little vague in his mind about method and procedure?

With best regards.

Yours very truly,
John C. Van Dyke

*Onteora Park*
*September 12, 1926*

Dear Mrs. Vanamee:

Thank you for your telegram. Am glad to hear the Hawthorne nomination is complete. He has received a good many honors, medals, and the like—more than I can remember or place, but I hope you were able to list them. That new (1925) *Dictionary of American Artists* (compiled by a Philadelphian whose name won't come to mind) should contain a pretty full account of him.

Carl Sandburg, sometime known as a sort of tramp poet (I never liked his poetry), has written a two-volumed *Lincoln* that I have read with much admiration. It should entitle him to election in the Institute. Do you know of any objection to him? I am also thinking of asking Louis Betts to propose for the Institute Steichen [two illegible names], those portrait painters. Again, is there any objection? Garland[72] has written Prof. William Ellery Leonard, of the University of Wisconsin (I think), asking if he will stand for the Institute on his "Two Lives." It is quite a long and fine poem. I was impressed with it.[73] But once again is there objection? I keep appealing to you because you know the inside history of these men, events, and happenings.

Thank you much.

Hastily,
John C. Van Dyke

Mrs. William Vanamee

• • •

72. Novelist Hamlin Garland, Van Dyke's fellow academy member and neighbor at the Onteora Club, recorded favorable reminiscences of Van Dyke. See Garland.

73. William Ellery Leonard's *Two Lives*. Leonard should not be lightly dismissed. He has an admirable ear for words and a skill with dramatic shifts; but, finally, his talent embroiders cliché. The concluding lines of his book-length poem read:

> I built her many a fire for love . . . for mirth . . . .
> (When snows were falling on our oaks outside,
> Dear, many a winter fire upon the hearth) . . .
> (. . . farewell . . . farewell . . . farewell . . . .)
> We dare not think too long on those who died,
> While still so many yet must come to birth.

In yet another irony, Van Dyke's tastes in poetry ran to the popular sentimentalism his own art criticism condemned. Van Dyke himself was a closet poet who, to his credit, had the wisdom not to appear often in print. For a sampling, see his *Autobiography:* "The Piazetta" (153–54), a creditable job; the less-so "Guinea Hens" (215); and the bathetic "Wild Geese" (215–16).

Hotel Telephone Nos. 253, 254
Office Telephone No. 255
The Great Eastern Hotel Ltd.
Telegrams
"Greastern Calcutta"
Codes
A B C 4W & 5W Editions, A1 and Bentley's

*Post Box 192*
*Calcutta*
*January 19, 1929*

Mrs. William Vanamee
American Academy of Arts and Letters
633 West 155th Street

My Dear Mrs. Vanamee:

Will you be a good angel once more and send these two little checks where they belong? I haven't been to the Authors Club in twenty years and don't know where or what the address of the new Club home.

I'm pretty well fed up on India and am leaving in a few days for Hong Kong and the Phillipines (or is it Philippines?) Miss May probably damned India for the wrong thing but certainly it deserves damning.[74]

Happy New Year to you!

Yours very truly,
John C. Van Dyke

• • •

74. Compare with the expanded thoughts on India and the Philippines in Van Dyke's *Autobiography* (196–201). Van Dyke traveled to every continent except Antarctica. His reactions often are unpredictable and inexplicable. Sometimes he will devote a whole book to celebrating a particular land that catches his fancy; at others he dismisses an entire country with an angry sentence or two.

*Onteora Club*
*Tannersville, N.Y.*
*September 24 [1930]*

Dear Mrs. Vanamee:

What, may I ask, are the duties of "Escort to Dr. del Campo" for November 13th and 14th?[75] If it is merely a matter of putting him up at a couple of clubs and finding him a seat on a platform, I might do it, but if I have to sit up all night on a roof garden then count me out. I'm not much of a night bird. And that reminds me that I am on the executive committee of the big pageant celebrating the 200th anniversary of New Brunswick at just that time and should be there.[76] Cortissoz who, I think, speaks Spanish would be better guidance and company. Try him and if every other fails you can always fall back on Garland, whom we all delighted to honor the other day.

Yours ever,
John C. Van Dyke

• • •

75. Dr. Cupertino del Campo, director of the National Museum of Argentina and delegate of the Instituto Cultural Argentina-Norte-Americano, was in town to promote Pan-American unity ("Pan-American Unity Urged").

76. New Brunswick received its founding charter in 1730 (Wall 17).

## BUTLER LIBRARY, COLUMBIA UNIVERSITY*

RUTGERS COLLEGE
and the
STATE UNIVERSITY OF NEW JERSEY
New Brunswick, New Jersey
Department of Fine Arts

*May 8, 1922*

Dear B.M.:[77]

Thank you very much for the handsome review in the *Times*.[78] You make me out such a remarkable dual personality that I have to rub my eyes to see if I am awake. But I am mighty glad to be reviewed by someone who sees what I am driving at. I am sure yours will be the only review to point out that my "nature study" is out of the ordinary—unique experiences. I have never written about robins on suburban lawns or woodchucks under Adirondack cabins. I never shot a skunk under the woodshed and made a chapter out of it. I don't despise the intimate study of the cockroach and the pinching bug. But all that has been done dozens of times. On the contrary, the big nature of the open spaces, the blue sky, the sea, the desert, etc., never has been done properly by anyone. Michelet,[79] Ruskin,[80] and others have made feeble shots at it by way of illustrating the vast superiority of man but they never had any proper experience in it or comprehension of it. The field is still unexplored. I have been looking into it for many years, but everything I have written about it has been rated "Dry." It hasn't contained the everlasting "human interest." The reader objects that I will talk about the sea instead of the man who is drowning and that I say my beatitudes to the desert mountains instead of blubbering over the tenderfoot dying of thirst in the valley below. I daresay my point of view is warped but my point is that I shouldn't be shot up because I do not write about the things of Burroughs or Thoreau or Jeffers. That's why I am so pleased with your recognition—that you "can't find a mate"

* Butler Library, Columbia University in the City of New York.

for my book. It really is unique though I am not denying that it may be uniquely bad.[81]

But thank you for your good words. I am glad to be your friend of forty years and proud of it into the bargain.

Yours ever,
John C. Van Dyke

• • •

77. In adulthood, James Brander Matthews dropped the use of his first name.

78. See Matthews's "Glad Nights and Days under the Blue Sky," a review of *The Open Spaces*.

79. Jules Michelet, French romantic writer and historian.

80. John Ruskin, English social theorist and aesthetician. Van Dyke's art theories owed a great deal to Ruskin (*Autobiography* 41, 115, 128, 234 n. 8).

81. As sales and reviews attest, Van Dyke's nature books hardly were "shot up," either by readers or critics. There's considerable truth in his comments about the popular nature writing of his day, but, beyond that, Van Dyke enjoyed thinking of himself as a lone rebel.

*New Brunswick, N.J.*
*February 5, 1924*

Dear Brander:

I am sure all your friends who saw the notices in the morning's newspapers feel a great sympathy for you in your loss of Mrs. Matthews. I am one of your friends, and I want you to know that I am very sorry you are bereaved and left alone. But more than that what can one say? I saw something of Mrs. Matthews years ago, and have always remembered her bright spirit and contagious laugh: but above all else I remember her great devotion to you. You will miss her greatly, and anything your friends may say will not make the longing less. But the friends would help you if they could, and they want you to feel that. What a helpless lot we are at just such times as this! All we can do is to stretch out a hand in this dark to say we are there.

I hope you keep well. And you must carry on. We all have to do that whether we like it or not.

Yours ever,
John C. Van Dyke

AVERY ARCHITECTURAL AND FINE ARTS LIBRARY, COLUMBIA UNIVERSITY
*Kenyon Cox Collection**

RUTGERS COLLEGE
New Brunswick, N.J.

*April 29, 1893*

Dear Cox:[82]

I'm frank to confess that I like your outline of a book on technical art better than my own. It is logical and sequential where mine is not. The divisions, for instance, of each chapter into the representative and the artistic is just exactly what has bothered me all along the line, but I hadn't wit enough to do it, and where at one time I had vaguely thought it out, I abandoned it as impractical for but this reason. The reason is that the public is a great ass of some booby and won't understand it and won't try to understand it. They'll wonder and wonder why the actual is not the artistic and find fault with you for making any distinction between nature and art.

Again the separation of line from aerial? [illegible word] perspective though quite just is something they won't grasp. The fact is the average person likes the crude, disjointed idea. He will grasp an illustration in argument but utterly fail in grasping its bearing on the argument. One used over and over again in Art for Art's Sake. I must [go] out of my way to [too] with clap-trap descriptions—any lacking good argument for the sake of holding the attention of the readers. I begin on Coln in order to get him into something on the start that would be halfway interesting. You must somehow catch your audience, else what is the use of writing a book at all? *How to Judge of a Picture* was the worst and yet the most successful book in its sales that I have ever written. I succeeded solely because it was a flinging together of scrappy ideas without head or tail.

* Avery Architectural and Fine Arts Library, Columbia University in the City of New York.

I should very much like to see such a book as you contemplate writing. It wouldn't interfere with mine because mine will be through selling before yours gets out. I wouldn't, however, let your logical system appear on the surface. Use it, but hide it. People have a horror of systems and logical sequences.

This, of course, on the supposition that you wish to appeal to the *public*—and I wouldn't appeal to any other audience. You might with something excellent for painters, but there are not enough of them to make it pay expenses if they all bought copies. Financially, there is no hope whatever in either your book or mine. I made something out of mine as lectures and finally published them because I lost my nerve and had to stop believing, and besides I have many other more interesting pictures in the [three illegible words] with illustrations. Brownell hath sold 1,500 copies. If mine does as well, I shall be satisfied. At ten percent you see that only means $200. I have never made out of art one tenth of the actual money I have put into it—never expect to. It is an interesting thing to write and think about as pastime, but I make my bread in other ways. The book is the very last resource in liberation. Even the *Evening Post* pays better.

However, I don't want to throw cold water on your scheme. Go ahead with it and write at odd times, and even if it doesn't pay financially it may in other ways. You have the advantage of having the material in your hand and will write it eventually. I should sincerely welcome such a book because I know it must be a good one.

Yours very truly,
John C. Van Dyke

Kenyon Cox, Esq.

• • •

82. Painter Kenyon Cox (1856–1919), a contributor of authoritative articles on art to national magazines.

## PRINCETON UNIVERSITY
## *Harrison S. Morris Papers**

*New Brunswick, N.J.*
*December 12, 1903*

Dear Mr. Morris:

I have asked Mr. Bernard Berenson, the well-known art critic, whom I beg to introduce herewith, to call upon you and ask your advice about how to see certain pictures in Philadelphia. I know you will be glad to help him in any way possible to you.[83]

Regards to you.

Yours very truly,
John C. Van Dyke

[a 3 x 5 card follows, bearing Van Dyke's handwriting]

*Harrison S. Morris, Esq.*
*Secretary*
*to the Penna. Academy of Fine Art*
*Philadelphia*

Introducing
Mr. Bernard Berenson

• • •

83. Box 130, Folder 33, Morris Papers, Princeton University Library. Although he was widely acknowledged in Van Dyke's time as an authority on the art of the Italian Renaissance, today many of the theories of Bernard Berenson (1865–1959) are held suspect.

* Manuscripts Division, Department of Rare Books and Special Collections, Princeton University Library. Published with permission of the Princeton University Library. Philadelphia industrialist, littérateur, and civic leader Harrison S. Morris (1856–1948) was a typical jewel in Van Dyke's orbit. A descendant of George Washington, poet, novelist, and arts editor of the *Ladies' Home Journal*, this longtime Van Dyke friend variously served as president of the Wharton Steel Company and as director of the Pennsylvania Academy of The Fine Arts, Philadelphia.

RUTGERS COLLEGE
and
SCIENTIFIC SCHOOL
The New Jersey College for the
Benefit of Agriculture and the Mechanic Arts
New Brunswick, N.J.

*June 19, 1906*

Dear Morris:

Thank you very much for your nice letter. That is the sort of a letter a fellow likes to receive—not because it is complimentary, necessarily, but because it comes from one who knows. The newspaper reviews[84] are silly and sloppy and the gush of one female acquaintance is something wonderful in its indiscriminate flair; so that one comes to value a word from those who know. Glad, indeed, that you like the book. I don't know what to make of it myself. It made me tired—that's all I know about it.

I don't see why you label your "Sea Library" "not for publication." Don't you think to publish it at all? It is first rate and should see the light. Of course, the subject is big—big for you as for me. That is what makes it attractive. We can't grasp it and hold it in the hollow of our hand as we would a marigold. That is perhaps where we fall down and bump ourselves.[85]

Well, at any rate, I shall tackle the sea once more, literally rather than artistically at that, too, on this Saturday morning. I'm off for Russia, where I may realize and then send you a bump—that is, if I am allowed in the country at all.

Good summer to you and "more power to your Elbow," as the Irish have it. Wish I could see you oftener than once a year.

Yours ever,
John C. Van Dyke

• • •

84. Of *The Opal Sea.* Box 130, Folder 33, Morris Papers, Princeton University Library.

85. Though the reference to Morris's "Sea Library" is obscure, it may be related to his *Masterpieces of the Sea. William T. Richards: A Brief Outline of His Life and Art*, published in 1912. An aficionado of the sea, Morris was a member of two yacht clubs.

RUTGERS COLLEGE
and
SCIENTIFIC SCHOOL
The New Jersey College for the
Benefit of Agriculture and the Mechanic Arts
New Brunswick, N.J.

*April 28, 1908*

Dear Morris:

Thank you very much for sending me the new volume, "Lyrics and Landscapes." I had read some of the poems before but I re-read the whole book last night and found it *very* good. You may think because I have been writing "How" books all my life that I know nothing about poetry; but I do. I served a long apprenticeship at it, and may return to it before I pass out. Just at present, however, there are too many things and people to be cussed off the face of the earth in plain prose. I send you my latest cussing under separate cover.[86] It is just a beginning. If I get any encouragement, I'll probably swear for the rest of my life. Regards to you.

Yours very truly,
John C. Van Dyke

• • •

86. Published in 1908, Van Dyke's *The Money God: Chapters of Heresy and Dissent Concerning Business Methods and Mercenary Ideals in American Life* blisters at American greed and stupidity while conveniently praising Van Dyke's friend Andrew Carnegie for his philanthropy. This is Van Dyke's most intemperate book.

RUTGERS COLLEGE
and
SCIENTIFIC SCHOOL
The New Jersey College for the
Benefit of Agriculture and the Mechanic Arts
New Brunswick, N.J.

*May 18 [1908]*[87]

Dear Morris:

Thank you ever so much for your letter. I don't care whether it's flattering or not; I like it. It induces one to spit on his hands and take a fresh hold—only it makes me curse to think that I can never get hold of anything by the head. All my life I have had things by the tail and been pulling them against the fur. As a result, the idea is always rumpled up and looks as though it had been killed with a club. But maybe that is the common experience.

Sorry; but I can't join your canoe party. Too busy. Besides, I'll have all the camping out I can stand this summer. Going West in a couple of weeks by way of the Canadian Rockies to the interior of Oregon where I hope to see some untouched country and catch some big salmon and trout.[88] Also to gather some further material for a book on the Mountains which I shall some day perpetrate, I think.[89]

Regards to you and good summer! Wish you would stop off here some day and see me.

Yours hastily,
John C. Van Dyke

• • •

87. Box 130, Folder 33, Morris Papers, Princeton University Library. The year is taken from the envelope following the letter in the collection, postmarked May 18, 1908.

88. Van Dyke likely was visiting his brother, Dr. Frederick Van Dyke, a physician in Grants Pass, Oregon.

89. *The Mountain*, a study of the aesthetics of mountain ranges around the world, would not appear until 1916.

[typewritten]

RUTGERS COLLEGE
New Brunswick, New Jersey

*September 22, 1909*

Harrison S. Morris, Esq.
The Annex, Milestown
Oak Lane Post Office
Phil., Penn.

Dear Morris:

All right about the Century. I will do what I can. It shouldn't be a very difficult job. Just back from Europe where I have been rowing with Pennell. Hope to see you soon.

Hastily yours,
John C. Van Dyke

[added by hand:] The Pennell Show opens at Keppel today. You should see it. Regards

J.C.VD.[90]

• • •

90. This letter and the following November 20, 1909, letter are located in Box 130, Folder 33, Morris Papers, Princeton University Library. This letter and the ones immediately following show Van Dyke at work doing one of the things he loved best, lobbying and jockeying politically to get a friend into one of the exclusive New York clubs of the era, in this case, the Century Club. It is notable behavior for a man who stated in *The Desert* that such trappings of "civilization" were "useless" and "contemptible" (200).

[typewritten]

RUTGERS COLLEGE
New Brunswick, New Jersey

*November 20, 1909*

Harrison S. Morris, Esq.
Oak Lane Post Office
Philadelphia, Pa.

Dear Morris:

I understand from a member of the Membership Committee of the Century that your name is not being acted upon by the Committee, because you have had no formal seconder. This is requisite. The seconder must send a formal letter to the Committee stating that he seconds your nomination. You better have some artist like Frederick Deilman do this for you. It should be done at once.

I wrote some weeks ago a letter for you.

Yours very truly,
John C. Van Dyke

[typewritten]

RUTGERS COLLEGE
New Brunswick, New Jersey

*May 17, 1910*

Harrison S. Morris
Oak Lane Post Office
Philadelphia, Pa.

Dear Morris:

Don't fret your soul about the Century matter. It will probably come out all right. The status of it is as follows: You were proposed by Will H. Low, but never formally and properly seconded. Fifteen or twenty coots, myself included, wrote their names in the book, and thought they were doing you great and signal service; but that had no effect on the Committee on Admissions.

They will not take cognizance of any proposal unless duly and formally seconded *by letter.* When I found out this situation, I duly and formally seconded you by letter. That was December, 1909. You are now formally posted as being proposed in December, 1909. It is the rule of the Committee not to consider any proposal until after six months have elapsed. You therefore would not come up for consideration until June or July and you won't come up then, because the Committee has held its last meeting for the summer and has adjourned until the fall. I do not doubt that you will be duly elected in the fall. In the meantime rest you should in peace and enjoy the green fields around Oak Lane.

Yours very truly,
John C. Van Dyke

[typewritten; carbon]

*May 14, 1920*

My Dear Van Dyke:

I have long had "American Painting and Its Tradition"[91] and have read in and in it [*sic*] now and then through a pretty busy life. Thus I have now grasped its purpose and message and I must thank you for a very useful record of American Art in its best estate. Of course, much of it is bound up with my life as it is with yours. I knew not Inness or Wyant, or Martin, but all the rest I have known and I was alert for what you would say of them as persons and painters.

I find nothing to disagree with and much that is supported by my own knowledge; and your inferences and conclusions seem well adapted. Perhaps I should have dwelt on the lack of general culture: reading and collateral education which is the hindrance to original thought and impulse amongst our painters of my day. You assign want of tradition—well, that too; but I think men like Chase, who never read a book, scarcely opened a newspaper, are not furnished for original conceptions. When even Alexander had to illustrate Pittsburgh in mural designs, his imagination threw off no sparks, and I've always felt a lack of humor in the mailed figure (of Andy?) popping out of the furnace. But I must say no mean word about the Well-Beloved![92]

I've just done a short paper on the John G. Johnson collection for *Scribner's*.[93] Do say what you think of my position. I've also dropped from my organ of mental gestation a novel called "Hannah Bye."[94] Are you appalled?

Yours ever,
Harrison S. Morris

• • •

91. Van Dyke's *American Painting and Its Tradition* is a long essay on such painters as Inness, Homer, Whistler, and Chase, all associated with impressionism, from about 1878 to 1915, and all central to Van Dyke's art preferences. Taking an ironic turn from his title, Van Dyke argues that there was little art tradition in the United States until men of this group modified styles learned during their apprenticeships in Europe.

92. A reference to John W. Alexander's mural work in the Carnegie Institute in Pittsburgh. Morris is taking a poke at Alexander and perhaps at Pittsburgh steel magnate Andrew Carnegie, too. According to Van Dyke, Alexander tells "the story of steel and labor. It is called the 'Apotheosis of Pittsburgh,' with the city personified by a knight in armor with a flaming sword in his hand" (*American Painting* 238).

93. See Morris's "The Art Collection of John G. Johnson."

94. In Morris's *Hannah Bye*, a sweet-souled Quaker girl comes in conflict both with her harsh mother and with Ruth Blake, Hannah's best friend, blinded by the wooing of a predatory male.

[typewritten; carbon]

*November 21, 1922*

Dr. John C. Van Dyke
Rutgers College
New Brunswick, New Jersey

My Dear Van Dyke:

I have been reading with a grin of satisfaction about the investigation of one Kaser, County Superintendent of Schools of Burlington County.[95]

I would like to add our experience to that of the others who have suffered. The Estate of Joseph Wharton, who was Mrs. Morris' father,[96] has a large tract in Burlington and Atlantic Counties, and there are remote settlements like Atsion, Sandy Ridge, and Tabernacle, where numerous children have failed to receive education during the past two years, because of the removal or closing of public schools. We have a perfectly equipped school at Atsion, with children to fill it, and this County Superintendent has decided the children must be transported to Indian Mills, considerable distance away, where a new school has been put up which will not accommodate all the children desiring education. In bad weather the transportation was not effective, and education much interrupted, and to us the whole system seemed to be fatal to enlightenment. Conditions are bad enough in South Jersey among the Pineys, and those who are inclined to go to school ought to be encouraged.

I could send you copies of my correspondence with Kaser, and his original replies, if you desired to have them.

Why don't I see something of you in New York or elsewhere? It is a great deprivation.

Yours truly,
[Harrison S. Morris; unsigned carbon]

• • •

95. This letter and the following November 23, 1922, letter are located in Box 130, Folder 33, Morris Papers, Princeton University Library. At the time, Van Dyke was a member of the New Jersey State Board of Education, and the exchange here shows yet another side of Van Dyke, his ability to take a public trust seriously. Morris is asking an inappropriate favor. His concern is not for children's education, as he purports, but for the smooth functioning of his huge estate. Located in the poor "cranberry counties" of southern New Jersey, it depended on transient labor during harvest time. To buck the consolidation plan in place and staff the small school on his property would ensure a steady supply of workers during the peak season. Van Dyke's response is swift, sympathetic, but firm. Sorry, he says in effect, I would like to help, but the larger good of public education comes first.

96. A wealthy industrialist of wide intellectual scope, Joseph Wharton was the founder of the famed Wharton School of Finance at the University of Pennsylvania. Morris, by the way, not only came into possession of the Wharton Estate through his father-in-law, he also succeeded him in the presidency of the Wharton Steel Company.

[typewritten]

STATE OF NEW JERSEY
State Board of Education
Trenton

*New Brunswick, New Jersey*
*November 23, 1922*

Mr. Harrison S. Morris
Liberty Building
Philadelphia, Pennsylvania

Dear Morris:

I have your letter about the Kaser appointment. Of course, there have been other letters along the same line and many others on the other side of the case. The crucial point is that the policy of consolidating schools is not Kaser's but that of the State Board of Education and the Commissioner of Education. Kaser is only an officer obeying instructions. For many years the cry in the State of New Jersey has been that the children in the one-room country school were not getting the same chance at education as those in the city schools. We tried to better this condition by a policy of consolidation, only to find almost every one against us because of some additional expense. The consolidation plan is not new in the State of New Jersey but is being installed in every state of the Union.

Of course, there will always be opposition to laying violent hands upon the little red schoolhouse. On the other hand, there is opposition when we do not lay hands upon it. The devil confronts us on one side and the deep sea on the other.

It is getting nearly time for some doings of the National Institute, and perhaps I shall be able to see you in New York. Trust that all goes well with you.

Yours very truly,
John C. Van Dyke

[typewritten; carbon]

*February 13, 1924*

Dr. John C. Van Dyke
Rutgers College
New Brunswick, N.J.

My Dear Van Dyke:

I am very much indebted to you, indeed, for sending me the papers relating to the attendance of school children at Atsion, N.J. The report made by the investigator who went there, was according to the facts. The attendance had been very irregular because the children could not be accommodated in the school at Indian Mills, and because of the conditions under which they were transported there. The bus was operated with open windows in the coldest weather, and children were made ill by this circumstance. Since the visit of your investigator the bus driver has been discharged and a new one installed, and it is hoped this will remedy that situation. There ought also to be covers provided for the children in cold weather, if they are obliged to go to Indian Mills, 4½ miles away, for instruction.

As a result of my letter to you there was a visit by a local official named Keyser [also spelled "Kaser" and "Kayser" in related correspondence], who stigmatized himself by telling our Superintendent, Mr. Etheridge, that the reason I wrote you was in dissatisfaction at the rise in the taxes on the Wharton Estate. As the taxes have not been raised, and they have always been paid without protest, this is, of course, merely a politician's falsehood. I wrote you because of the rather galling conditions covering education prevailing down there in the essential business of schooling the growing generation. Our belief is that the official who made the assertion is one of the contributing causes to the unfavorable state of things.

I wish to goodness I could see you oftener, one of the reasons being that I should deeply enjoy a talk on your Rembrandt book, which I entirely endorse.[97]

Yours ever,
[Harrison S. Morris; unsigned carbon]

• • •

97. Aware that Van Dyke had seen through his scheme to locate a school near his landholding, Morris appears to take this occasion to insinuate himself back into Van Dyke's good graces by justifying his previous requests concerning the Burlington County Schools. And in something of a non sequitur in the last paragraph of his letter, Morris allies himself with Van Dyke in the uproar raking the art world caused by Van Dyke's controversial *Rembrandt and His School*, published a few months earlier. Morris was one of Van Dyke's few committed supporters in the fray.

Yet ingratiation may not have been the motive, at least the entire motive. In *Confessions in Art*, Morris shows himself an enthusiast for Van Dyke's critical judgments (231).

RUTGERS COLLEGE
and the
STATE UNIVERSITY OF NEW JERSEY
New Brunswick, New Jersey

*November 21, 1924*

Mr. Harrison S. Morris
Oake Lane P.O.
Philadelphia, Pa.

Dear Morris:

My statement to you last night about my position on the question of admitting women to the Institute was not quite accurate.

Perhaps I overstated it because I wished you to understand that I favored the admission of women, but, thinking it over on the train last night, I remembered that I had not voted for Miss Repplier on the technical ground that the Council should not be forced to report the nomination when the question had not been decided by the Institute. That position was afterwards adopted by the Council, namely, that the Council would not report the names of women until so authorized by the general body of the Institute.

This is of no particular consequence, but I wish no misunderstanding. Words flew fast and furious last night, and perhaps, under the circumstances, you will pardon the error of statement. Now that you are on the Council, I hope I shall see more of you than heretofore.

Yours very truly,
John C. Van Dyke

*Sunset Heights*
*Asheville, N.C.*
*February 15 [1925]*

Dear Harrison Morris:

I fear I shall not be able to attend that wedding for the reason that I am down here at Asheville taking a cure for a damaged lung, but I rejoice at the wedding which means that some people are well and happy and that after all "all's right with the world." Will you express that sentiment to the bride and groom with my best wishes for long life, *health*, and happiness?

I am not very hard hit and am promised "long life" and a chance to die from the kick of a mule or something equally as bad.[98]

Regards to you and Mrs. Morris.

Yours ever,
John C. Van Dyke

• • •

98. Box 130, Folder 33, Morris Papers, Princeton University Library. Notice that Van Dyke manages to bring the topic of conversation back around to his health, which is a major theme of his letter writing. As for Sunset Heights, see his *Autobiography* (181–82). An envelope included after this letter bears a cancellation from Asheville of February 16, 1925, providing the year of the letter.

[typewritten; carbon]

*November 24, 1924*

Dr. John C. Van Dyke
Rutgers College
New Brunswick, New Jersey

Dear Van Dyke:

It was not necessary, though very pleasant, to hear from you on the subject of that stimulating debate. I suppose some people think there is heat in it; I find only light.

I was told that Hill considered your position correct and my original one incorrect, but I am quite sure of one thing: that the affairs of that delightful Club of distinguished authors and artists should not be messed by an appeal to rigid parliamentary form. I, and a lot with me, can see no reason why we should not be allowed to debate in a friendly way the whole question of the right of the Institute to elect women. Mere obstruction is not friendly and is never a prevailing method of promoting a cause. Sooner or later it goes down.

I shall meet you now in the Council and we can there talk it over frankly without obstructing tactics and I am sure we shall reach a most amiable conclusion.

Always warmly yours,
[Harrison S. Morris; unsigned carbon]

THEOLOGICAL SEMINARY
New Brunswick, New Jersey
Sage Library

*May 15, 1929*

Harrison S. Morris, Esq.
Oak Lawn, Phila.

Dear Morris:

Thank you much for the poems, the happy inscription, and the good thought of me. I am glad to have them all. And glad to see that your hand hasn't lost its cunning. I have read the poems and think them quite your best, though you hark back a long way and sound a little sad.[99] I am also writing my recollections of Abraham Lincoln and the Civil War. There is nothing left but the past to write about. But we will keep on coming, like your Grand Army, until there isn't a son of a gun left.[100]

Yours ever,
John C. Van Dyke

• • •

99. Harrison S. Morris, *Martial Notes of the Old War and the New.*

100. See the first chapter of Van Dyke's *Autobiography*, "Lincoln in 1861" (11–16).

## FROM THE PRIVATE COLLECTION OF ALAN VAN DYKE GOLDEN*

RUTGERS COLLEGE
and the
STATE UNIVERSITY OF NEW JERSEY
New Brunswick, New Jersey
Department of Fine Arts

*January 26 [1923]*[101]

Dear The:

I have your letter but hardly know what to say about coming out this spring. I am so full of work that it seems impossible to get away. The reasoning is that there is no one left who knows how to do anything or is even willing to work. My Rembrandt book is in the press but I have to tell the d—— printers just what type, caps., page, paper, etc. I will have. There isn't a printer alive that knows his job. We have two millions in buildings in course of erection, but I have to tell the architects just what to do.[102] In putting up those buildings at Trenton we are paying bricklayers $13.50 a day, *and board, and railway fare* for laying 400 bricks a day according to union rules. Well, all life is just like that everywhere in this Eastern region. The result is that people who know [how] and are willing to work are in great demand. Of course I might walk off and tell everyone to go to the dev— but that isn't quite the right thing to do, either. But we shall see. If I decide to summer in America (and I may have to do that on account of the European situation), I shall almost surely come West. Just now the Legislature is in session and I have plenty of quarrels there. In the Spring the Rembrandt book is coming out and there are mutterings about that already. I may find the rancho [*sic*] a good place to retreat to. Health seems about the same, though I get badly bored by increasing age. I don't like it. Between govern-

* Courtesy Mr. Alan Van Dyke Golden. The grandnephew of John C. Van Dyke, Mr. Golden was born on the Van Dyke ranch, near Daggett, California, owned by John's brother Theodore, to whom the following letter is addressed.

ment and a bad throat, I may have to quit and take a week's job of carrying swill to the hogs as an occupation. But we shall see.

I wrote Dix about six weeks ago all the news I had on trip.[103]

Yours,
JCVD

• • •

101. The year of the letter is taken from the envelope, dated January 27, 1923.

102. The building construction and the mention of the state legislature likely refer to Van Dyke's service on the New Jersey State Board of Education.

103. Dix Van Dyke was Theodore's son. For Dix's colorful version of life on the ranch, see *Daggett: Life in a Mojave Frontier Town.*

## GARDNER A. SAGE LIBRARY, NEW BRUNSWICK THEOLOGICAL SEMINARY*

SIX HUNDRED AND FORTY FIFTH AVENUE

*[no date]*

Dear Mr. Van Dyke:

I go south on Friday, and while the house is open, the front door is closed.

If you will telephone my butler Deacon—752 Plaza—he will let you in any time you call.

Sincerely yours,
H. C. Frick

[penciled in by Van Dyke:] Henry C. Frick—millionaire
[and then added:] steel partner of Carnegie

* Property of the New Brunswick Theological Seminary Archives, Gardner A. Sage Library.

THE CARNEGIE STEEL COMPANY, LIMITED
General Offices, Carnegie Building
Pittsburgh, PA
H. C. Frick
Chairman, Board of Managers

*September 24, 1895*

My Dear Sir:

I am just in receipt of yours of the 23rd.

Beg to hand you herewith my check for one hundred and fifty dollars ($150.00).

Am glad to get a picture by Mr. Crane, and have no doubt it will prove satisfactory.[104] If not, I will avail myself of your kindness in agreeing to have him paint another.

I had the pleasure of a visit from Mr. Thomson last evening, and glad of an opportunity of showing him what few pictures I have purchased.[105]

If I do not have the pleasure of meeting you before, trust I will have in this City at the opening of the Carnegie Library.

Yours very truly,
H. C. Frick

To: Mr. John C. Van Dyke
Care Rutgers College
New Brunswick, N.J.

P. S. Please have pictures sent by Adams Express to me at Homewood Station, P.R.R., Allegheny County, Pa.

• • •

104. This likely is the artist Bruce Crane mentioned by Van Dyke in his letter to Carnegie dated April 3, 1893, in the Library of Congress correspondence, above.

105. At the time, Frank Thomson (1841–1899) was first vice-president of the Pennsylvania Railroad. He would become president in 1897. An art connoisseur and collector, he was Van Dyke's dearest friend. See Van Dyke's *Autobiography* (73–76, 104–5, 117, 227 n. 5).

H. C. FRICK
Pittsburgh, PA

*April 16, 1897*

My Dear Mr. Van Dyke:

Replying to your favor of the 15th.

It is my present intention to be in New York the greater part of next week, arriving there Monday morning.

Many kind thanks for your kind invitation to dine. As I will have my family with me, I may not be able to accept that invitation, but will write you after reaching New York, and would be glad to have a view of the Rousseau, and other pictures, of your friend, Mr. Fuller.[106]

Yours very truly,
H. C. Frick

To: Mr. John C. Van Dyke
New Brunswick, N.J.

• • •

106. Van Dyke's *Autobiography* recalls traveling "with my friend William H. Fuller (at first a collector of old English pictures but latterly an admirer of Monet) to Giverney and saw Monet in his garden" (80–81). Van Dyke then reviews Fuller's career as a collector and notes that he bought Rousseau's *Charcoal Burner's Hut* for "$15,000 and thought he had paid too much for it, though a few years later it sold for $65,000"—the latter a huge sum in those days (81).

[typewritten, except as noted]

SKIBO CASTLE
Ardgay, [Dornoch—crossed out] N.B.

*June 29, 1898*

[To the left of the letterhead, written slantwise, in what appears to be Van Dyke's hand, is "This is the letter in which A.C. wrote in pencil to give McLuckie all the money he wanted and to 'rub this out.' See {Carnegie's} *Autobiography* 237." An arrow points to a message written in the left-hand margin. The words are erased, but the last line is readable. It says "rub this out."]

My dear Professor,

Sorry you are getting to be one of the capitalistic class—too bad. We are looking forward to the arrival of the book you have sent us. Sorry we are not to see you here this year, as we fully expected you to come. I think you promised to do so if I recollect, but next year surely we are to have the pleasure of a visit. We told Lady Waterlow she might expect to find you here. There is plenty of fishing at Skibo, salt and freshwater, and you will like it for many reasons, although we have nothing quite so rugged as the scenery at Laggan. We are all well and delighted to hear of your success. Shall see you in October, when we hope this petty war will be over.[107] Frank Thomson is behaving badly to us—so I hear from Frick and Schwab. I wish you would talk to him; he will listen to a capitalist. [added by hand] altho unmindful of poor manufacturers upon his line.[108]

Always very truly yours,
Andrew Carnegie

John C. Van Dyke, Esq.

Nerzoe [Hertzog] Hall, New Brunswick, N.C. ["C" crossed out and "J" added with pen]

• • •

107. The Spanish-American War. In a rare declaration of his political sentiments, Van Dyke voiced his opposition to it (*Autobiography* 116). For his part, though an advocate of world peace, Carnegie did not hesitate to profit from the armaments industry.

108. At the time, entrepreneurs Henry C. Frick and Charles M. Schwab were Carnegie allies. As mentioned earlier, by then Frank Thomson was president of the Pennsylvania Railroad.

Concerning the difficulty with Thomson referred to in the letter: "Of the railroad on which he [Carnegie] had spent his apprentice years, and for which his affection was almost filial, he had become the largest single patron, his monthly freight bills pouring enormous sums into its coffers, yet it was using its monopoly to squeeze him to the final dollar. Several of his boyhood friends—Frank Thomson . . . and George B. Roberts—had for many years been remorselessly active in applying the screws" (Hendrick 2: 24).

[typewritten]

ANDREW CARNEGIE
5 West 51st Street
New York

*February 10, 1899*

Dear Mr. Van Dyke:

We are all glad to hear that good sense prevails at last, but it is a pity you are not going to Florida instead. I am going on Monday next.[109]

Very truly yours,
Andrew Carnegie

John C. Van Dyke, Esq.,
Rutgers College, New Brunswick, N.J.

[handwritten:] Don't miss Skibo this summer. You can't stay in California in hot weather. A.C.

• • •

109. It is unclear precisely what "good sense" had prevailed over, but in this letter Carnegie is expressing disappointment that his and Van Dyke's vacation plans had not coincided better.

THE TUSKEGEE NORMAL AND INDUSTRIAL INSTITUTE
For the Training of
Colored Young Men and Women
Tuskegee Institute, Alabama

*May 11, 1912*

My Dear Mr. Van Dyke:

We are making just now a special effort to raise $20,000 for the work of this institution by getting a number of our people to give one dollar each. You have been selected as one of the persons to be appealed to.

Of course, if you care to give more than a dollar, we shall be glad to have you do so. We shall be very grateful for anything you may send.

Enclosed you will find a blank to be filled out and a return envelope. The money can be sent in the form of stamps, cash, money order, or check. You will receive prompt receipt from our Treasurer.

Please let us hear from you at once.

Yours very truly,
Booker T. Washington
Principal[110]

• • •

110. Unfortunately, there is no record of how Van Dyke responded to this request.

HOTEL MARIE ANTOINETTE
Broadway 66th to 67th Street
New York

Cher monsieur,

Merci de votre jolie lettre, qui m'a particulièrement touché. Pardon d'avoir tardé à y répondre, au milieu de mon surmenage actuel.

A vous bien cordialement,
Pierre Loti

Heureux de savoir que mes livres sont [?] jusque dans du désert américain—

[penciled in by Van Dyke:] author of "Le Pêcheur d'Islande"
[and:] Pierre Loti author "Madame Chrisanthème," "Le Pêcheur d'Islande," etc. Oct 14, 1912

HOTEL MARIE ANTOINETTE
Broadway 66th to 67th Street
New York

Dear Sir,

Thank you for your nice letter that has touched me deeply. Excuse me for having taken so long to answer, as I am currently swamped with work.

Sincerely yours,
Pierre Loti

[handwritten:] Happy to know that my books are available [?] even in the American desert—[111]

• • •

111. This thank-you note establishes an important connection between two desert writers. Wildly decadent and wildly popular, French novelist Pierre Loti (1850–1923) was in New York City during 1912 to watch rehearsals for one of his plays. Van Dyke's *The Desert* may owe much of its lush romance to Loti's earlier writings about deserts. See Wild, "Viewing America's Deserts, Part 1: John C. Van Dyke and the French Connection."

WOODROW WILSON
38 W. State Street
Trenton, N.J.

*November 14, 1912*

My Dear Mr. Van Dyke:

Thank you very much for your message. It has been a matter of great pride with me during the last few months that the men who lead in the college world should have come in such generous numbers to my support, and it is delightful to me to think that possibly my success in this election will give the country a new conception of the relation of the colleges to public life. Too few have appreciated, I think, how near the college really lies to the public.[112]

Sincerely yours,
Woodrow Wilson

John C. Van Dyke
New Brunswick, N.J.

• • •

112. At the time of this letter, Governor Woodrow Wilson of New Jersey had just been elected to be the 28th president of the United States. Though Wilson was a Democrat and Van Dyke from a staunchly Republican family, Van Dyke says in his *Autobiography* that he and Wilson had been "very friendly" for a number of years previous to this letter (155). The good will is evidenced by Governor Wilson's appointment of Van Dyke to New Jersey's Board of Education in 1911. With Van Dyke, personal loyalties tended to outweigh politics.

TWO EAST NINETY-FIRST STREET
New York

*[November 1915]*[113]

My Dear Professor Van Dyke:

I was much disappointed at missing you this afternoon. I came downstairs just as your motor was leaving the drive. I was detained upstairs playing games with Mr. Carnegie, and when he learned you were here, he was most anxious to see you, and he was very disappointed when he learned you had gone.

On Thursday next Mr. Carnegie will be 80 years old, and I am inviting a few of his intimate friends to come in at a quarter before five o'clock to greet him. His strength is not yet fully returned, and the Doctor will only permit him to remain downstairs a short while. I know it will give him so much pleasure to see you. I do hope you may be able to come in at that time.

With kindest greetings, believe me,

Very sincerely yours,
Louise W. Carnegie

Sunday

• • •

113. The year of Carnegie's eightieth birthday.

EDWARD E. AYER
Railway Exchange Building
Chicago

*February 9, 1916*

Dear Mr. Van Dyke:

Mrs. Ayer and I are anticipating with the greatest pleasure the volume which you have in the press on The Mountain, and please do start that Blue Sky right away.

I have a very dear friend, Mr. Benjamin Winchell, who is Vice-President and Traffic Manager of the Union Pacific and is crossing the desert every little while. About a week ago, I presented him your Desert. He said he sat up until two o'clock in the morning reading it and was anxious to go on the Desert again. He had often recognized the feeling that you expressed but never had known how to express it himself or to put it together.

Last year the Outlook had heard something of my work through a mutual friend in New York and asked me to be interviewed. I supposed they wanted to find out a little of the mode and methods of a very unfortunate man who never had had the advantages of a college education and how he got on. I am taking the liberty of sending you the Outlook of August 25th, and you will find the article on Page 997.[114] I certainly tried to steer him away from myself as much as possible and to make him familiar with the tremendous work going on by so many men in our beloved city. I should not have presumed to send you this article if it had not been the friendly tone of yours of the 22nd ult.

Mrs. Ayer and I will be on the Deserts south west of Tucson, then over the Imperial Valley of California by Auto in about a month. Of course, we take you with us.

Yours very sincerely,
Edward E. Ayer

Mr. John C. Van Dyke
New Brunswick, N.J.

• • •

114. Without being cloying, Donald Wilhelm's "A Lumberman Bibliophile" celebrates the frontier derring-do of a youthful Ayer in the West and lauds Ayer the mature businessman for his civic leadership. A director of various museums, fine-minded and pleasant-natured, Ayer, indeed, had a large soul.

B. F. STURTEVANT COMPANY
General Office and Works
Hyde Park
Boston, Mass.
34 Oliver Street
Boston, Mass.

*January 3, 1917*

Prof. J. C. Van Dyke
New Brunswick, N.J.

My Dear Prof. Van Dyke:

A plan is under way to secure for a Memorial in behalf of National Prohibition the signatures of one thousand men of eminence in American life. Among those to be appealed to will be manufacturers, bankers, railway presidents, university leaders, scientists, physicians, labor leaders, editors, and men in public life. It is hoped that this demonstration will have a weighty influence in securing wide public support to the policy of alcohol prohibition.

The work of securing the names will be undertaken by a subcommittee of the Committee of Sixty, under the guidance of Professor Irving Fisher of Yale. The draft of the declaration to be signed is enclosed. Important names have already come in. We should be deeply gratified to have the support of your influential signature in initiating this movement. We can give you the best assurances that it will be put through with judgment and tact.[115]

With sincere regards,

Faithfully yours,
Eugene Foos

[penciled in by Van Dyke:] Governor Foos of Mass.

• • •

115. Though in attempts to remedy his health problems Van Dyke tried various diets, and at one point became a vegetarian, he drank and smoked, at least occasionally. There is no evidence that he was a supporter of prohibition.

JOSEPH S. FRELINGHUYSEN<br>
Raritan, New Jersey<br>
Telephone 249 Somerville<br>
111 William Street, New York<br>
Telephone 5850-John

*February 2, 1917*

Dr. John C. Van Dyke
c/o Rutgers College
New Brunswick, N.J.

Dear Sir:

I thank you for your letter of January 27th.

I will not send the letter to Mr. McDonald because I do not think it would help the situation any. I was simply appealing for this man on account of his children. Possibly you are right, and extreme punishment should be enforced in this case.

I have no authority in the matter and have only been butting in without really any reasonable grounds for it. I always decide these matters from the heart instead of upon the merits of the case.

Very sincerely yours,<br>
Joseph Frelinghuysen

[penciled in by Van Dyke:] Joseph S. Frelinghuysen,
U.S. Senator from N.J.[116]

• • •

116. Joseph S. Frelinghuysen had not been sworn in as a U.S. senator yet. He had been elected in November 1916 and did not take office until April 5, 1917, so at the time, Van Dyke would have been asking for his influence on the state level. An extensive search of local New Brunswick newspapers has failed to uncover the specific case Van Dyke refers to here, but this note indicates that he feels comfortable calling upon powerful political men in the state when so compelled.

*The Newark Ledger*
237 Washington Street
Telephone Market 351
Newark, N.J.
L. T. Russell, Publisher

*October 10, 1920*

Dear Professor Van Dyke:

I suppose you are now back again in your Sage Library, writing a new colorful book. I liked your Colorado volume.[117]

I have recently been appointed Literary Editor of the above paper. I write book reviews and anything else I am minded to. If you are getting any work out soon, I'd be glad to hear about it, as I shall want to give it notice. (I suppose that you have written so many books that you do not care whether or not you receive any write-ups!)[118]

My book of poems has been delayed somewhat, but my publishers inform me that the volume will appear shortly. As soon as it appears, I shall send you a copy.

If you have any suggestions regarding the betterment of my Literary Page, I'd be much obliged to you.

Hoping to hear from you soon, I am,

Cordially yours,
Louis Ginsberg ('18)

[stationery footer:] Only morning newspaper in industrial center with a million population

• • •

117. *The Grand Canyon of the Colorado* (1920).

118. Quite to the contrary, both Van Dyke's personal Scrapbook at the Sage Library and a box in the Faculty Dead Files in Special Collections, the Alexander Library at Rutgers, containing voluminous clippings by and about Van Dyke, show that he fed on publicity. Van Dyke enjoyed applause from the public he despised. Note his antics recorded in his *Autobiography* (180–81), concluding with his statement: "Vanity is at the heart of us all. We are easily flattered. We may know that and yet still be pleased by the wish to flatter" (181).

JAMES BERTRAM
522 Fifth Avenue

*October 20, 1921*

Dear Dr. Van Dyke:

As we passed through New Mexico and Arizona on the way East this summer and saw the desert for the first time, you may imagine such names as Taos recalled many incidents in which you were prominent—the kidnapping threat, the "damned white of Andy" story, etc., not to speak of your word pictures of that unique region. I brought back all of the literature, being full of the idea of spending a few weeks there next summer out of the beaten track, after a consultation I hope to have with you some time before next season.

I have given an introduction to you to a very charming lady, Mrs. Henry Howard of Boston, who is about to send her son West for a few months setting up before entering college. Mrs. Howard and her husband have done so much for the country during the war, and are still, that I do not pass by any opportunity to be of service to her, and I bespeak from you any advice you can give Mrs. Howard about where and how the boy ought to go, which no one is more qualified to give than you. After a talk with me, they are quite taken with the idea of New Mexico.

Yours sincerely,
Jas Bertram[119]

Dr. John C. Van Dyke
New Brunswick, N.J.

• • •

119. James Bertram was Andrew Carnegie's secretary. His first paragraph only briefly lifts the veil on the intricate private lives and intrigues of the wealthy, rarely recorded and then more easily hidden than today. The "damned white of Andy" story refers to the unseemly McLuckie affair discussed in the introduction and in Carnegie's *Autobiography* (235–39). The "kidnapping threat" is yet another mystery in the several surrounding Van Dyke and Carnegie. There is no reference to it in the public record of either man's life.

MISS HELEN FRICK
Pittsburgh, Pennsylvania
New York Address:
1 East 70th Street

*February 27, 1922*

My Dear Mr. Van Dyke:

Although the collection of photographs we are compiling is only in its early stages of development and is not generally accessible, I would be very glad indeed to have you call some morning at your convenience, in order to judge how useful you may find it.

I fear it will be some time before we are able to show you an adequate collection of reproductions representing the artists you mention in your letter, but the best way to prove this is by your coming to see for yourself.

Will you kindly telephone ahead, so that I may have the pleasure of being here when you call?

Sincerely yours,
Helen C. Frick

Mr. John C. Van Dyke
Rutgers College
New Brunswick, New Jersey

6 Kirkland Road
Cambridge, Massachusetts

*October 5, 1924*

My Dear Mr. Van Dyke,

Thank you for the notice of *Democracy and Leadership* from *The Morning Post.* It had already reached me through another channel, but I appreciate your intention all the same. As a matter of fact, the English reviewers have dealt more mercifully with the book thus far than those in this country.

Sincerely yours,
Irving Babbitt[120]

• • •

120. Irving Babbitt (1865–1933) was associated with the New Humanism movement advocating classical moderation. At the time of this letter, he was a professor of French literature at Harvard.

BOWDOIN COLLEGE
Brunswick, Maine

*October 24, 1924*

My Dear Mr. Van Dyke,

In connection with the course on the history of modern painting which I give here, I have been studying your *Rembrandt and His School*—am, in fact, making it the basis of a complete revision of my consideration of Rembrandt; and, if I may do so without trespassing unduly on your time and patience, I should like to ask some questions about attribution of certain works, and particularly about the "dragged stroke."[121] It seems to me, though I am altogether without experience as an executant, that this simple phrase ought to be quite clear. I should say this stroke would be one made with a flat brush, larger or smaller, held flatwise or edgewise, applied rather heavily than lightly, and leaving a slightly striated rather than a smooth texture. But I find, in talking the matter over with such executants as are at hand—all amateurs, to be sure—a great variety of opinion in the matter. If you will enlighten me finally, I shall be very grateful; and if you will permit me to ask the further questions as to attribution, I shall be extremely glad to do so.

I want also to tell you that I find your book profoundly interesting and illuminating, and am placing it first amongst the reference works which my students use. I congratulate you upon it, and am,

Yours appreciatively,
Henry E. Andrews

Professor John C. Van Dyke
Rutgers College
New Brunswick, N.J.

• • •

121. This and the following piece probably were two of the few fan letters Van Dyke received in response to the book.

BOWDOIN COLLEGE
Brunswick, Maine

*October 29, 1924*

Dear Professor Van Dyke,

I thank you most heartily for your very prompt and very interesting reply to my question about the dragged brush stroke, and for letting me go ahead with my further questions about attributions.

Of course, the proper answer to the query about the brush stroke is in the picture, the actual execution, and I hope and plan before many years to be able to study the works themselves. Meantime, I want to come as near an understanding, imaginatively, as possible. Specimens of Rembrandt's technique, however, don't exist in this part of the world, though we have some drawings attributed to him, and your help is very edifying. In this connection, it isn't, perhaps, too late to ask about the "plated into place" which you use, along with "dragged" on p. 30. I should understand this plating to consist in a series of weaving strokes. Is it something like that? And is anybody in particular, so far as you know, the author of the phrase "gray period"?

It has been one of my cherished hopes that you might some day come to Brunswick. It would be a great pleasure to me to have you see what we have here, though perhaps not thrillingly profitable to you. I am glad to hear that you are wrestling with the Rembrandt etchings, and look forward to your conclusions with the greatest interest. Is it true also, as I have heard much less definitely—I can't, in fact, recall just when or how—that you are going, some day to publish a work on Rubens? Whether or no, I should like to stand beside you while you look at our "Rubens" here.[122]

Sincerely yours,
Henry E. Andrews

• • •

122. Van Dyke published no full-length study of Rubens.

FREDERICK LESLIE RANSOME
Economic Geologist
University of Arizona
Tucson, Arizona

*July 27, 1925*

My Dear Dr. Van Dyke:

On returning to Tucson for a few days from Butte, Montana, I found your note of July 18. It was very pleasant to have you turn to me in your dire distress.

To save your time, I have sent your note directly to Dr. Geo. Otis Smith, Director of the U.S. Geological Survey, Washington, D.C., and have asked him to have the maps sent to you, if available. I hope that he will send them with his compliments, but if he can not legally do this, there may be a charge of a few cents for the maps.[123]

[One line obscured by glue.] . . . over snowdrifts and wading icy streams in the lovely country just north of Yellowstone Park and the change to July weather is rather abrupt.

A year ago, I resigned from the U.S. Geological Survey and am now teaching geology at the University of Arizona. Should the charms of the desert (in any months save June, July, and August) draw you to Arizona, it would be a real pleasure both to me and to Mrs. Ransome to have you share our house and see something of the country near Tucson.

With cordial regard, I am,

Sincerely yours,
F. L. Ransome

• • •

123. Van Dyke fancied himself a keen amateur geologist who could outwit experts in their explanations of landforms. Hence, several of his books, such as *The Desert*, *The Mountain*, and *The Grand Canyon* contain large patches of theorizing about the earth's formation. Van Dyke's request for geological maps here probably arises from this motive.

STATE OF NEW JERSEY
State Board of Education
34 Pine Street
New York City

*September 15, 1925*

Dr. John C. Van Dyke
New Brunswick, New Jersey

Dear Dr. Van Dyke:

At our Board meeting last Saturday, I was informed that the Supreme Court sustained you and reversed me in the Mansfield township case, which you will doubtless remember.[124] At my request, Mr. Strahen has sent me copies of the Court's Opinion, one of which I enclose herewith. Please keep it as an evidence of your victory. It has just arrived, and I have had no opportunity to read it, but no matter what it says, I shall stick to my belief that I was right, though my natural chagrin is much alleviated by the fact that *you* have been held to be right.

I was very glad to hear from Mr. Murray that you are back at work again, and I only wish that you would get the Governor to reappoint you to the board. We have missed you more than you realize. If your travels bring you into my vicinity, won't you come in and see me?

Faithfully yours,
Oscar W. Jeffery

• • •

124. Appointed by Governor Woodrow Wilson, a man committed to cleaning up the horrendous corruption in his state, Van Dyke served on the New Jersey State Board of Education, 1911–1924. Van Dyke's *Autobiography* mentions the people in this letter and recounts the earnest but gentlemanly atmosphere prevailing among board members: "all might be foes over the board table but were friends at table" (160).

DAVENPORT HOTEL
L. M. Davenport, President
Spokane, USA

*October 5, 1925*

John C. Van Dyke
The National Institute of Arts and Letters

My Dear Sir:

I have been on the list of the National Institute for a long time, but for the most of that time was out of New York, and there was no special way to show my devotion.

I am sending you under separate cover a portfolio of my drawings issued first in 1910 and most of them done 1905–1910. Forty of these were recently incorporated in my *Illustrated Collected Poems*—issued by the Macmillan Company, May 19, 1925. For the history of the drawings, which I have always miscalled the Quillpage Magazine, I refer you to Farado Taft and Hamlin Garland.[125] In 1910, Hamlin Garland made me a member of the Cliff Dweller's Club, Chicago, on the strength of them, and I think it was largely through the memory of this first event that he subsequently used all his influence and secured for me the honor of a membership in The National Institute of Arts and Letters. To celebrate, as it were, the final issue of these poor drawings in official form, I have printed a special edition of 200 of them disguised as The Quillpage Magazine as heretofore, and have sent 40 of them to forty members of the Institute. I hope this may be preliminary to getting acquainted. I urge as my sponsor from of old, Hamlin Garland, who at one time—that is, in 1910, scattered this same magazine in practically this form with these same cuts—all over Chicago. I hope it adds to the gaiety, not the depression, of the Nation, the 48 states, and The National Institute of Arts and Letters.

Most Sincerely,
Vachel Lindsay[126]

• • •

125. This "Quillpage Magazine" was never registered with the Library of Congress. However, the illustrations Lindsay refers to do indeed exist, as he notes, in the first illustrated edition of his collected poems of 1925.

Both the poetry and the artwork appear somewhat dated in their eccentricity, as, for instance, the frontispiece of the book, "Map of the Universe Issued in 1909," which shows various celestial bodies emanating from a futuristic city, all of which is bordered by Phoenician hieroglyphics.

126. Poet Vachel Lindsay (1879–1931) is still remembered for his "General William Booth Enters into Heaven," a rollicking paean written after the death of the Salvation Army's founder. Lindsay and his followers were so taken by the marching rhythm Kipling and other balladists had restored to verse, that when they composed, it is said, they "pounded on the table / hard as they were able."

CHARLES SCRIBNER'S SONS
Publishers
Fifth Avenue at 48th Street
New York

*March 5, 1926*

My Dear Professor Van Dyke:

In these days when there is so much unlovely writing, it is a delight to find a book such as *The Meadows*, and I want to tell you what pleasure you have given at least one who likes the country, and who likes to read about it when the appreciation is so sympathetic and satisfying as yours. I have spent two delightful afternoons over your book, and I hope that it is no intrusion for me to let you know how finely you have captured the spirit of the meadows, especially in the winter.

It has not always been so, but now I am living in the city and have to content myself with an occasional walk in the early morning through Central Park, and I have been surprised by more birds and different trees than I used to think throve in New York.

Sometime when you are here at Scribner's, won't you stop in and see me at one of the corners of the fifth floor?

Yours cordially,
W. D. Howe

Professor John C. Van Dyke
Rutgers College
New Brunswick, N.J.

[penciled in by Van Dyke:] W. D. Howe, Author

BURTON J. HENDRICK
285 Madison Avenue
New York

*February 2, 1927*

Dear Professor Van Dyke,

I am writing this note to let you know that Mrs. Andrew Carnegie has placed in my hands all the letters and personal papers of her husband as materials for a complete, authorized biography. The book will describe Mr. Carnegie's career in all its phases—business, economic, educational, literary, and philanthropic—as well as give an intimate portrait of the man. I am asking all Mr. Carnegie's friends and correspondents to send me any of his letters they may have received and preserved for possible use in his biography. Your kindness in sending to me (to this address) any letters from Mr. Carnegie in your possession would be much appreciated. I can assure you that all letters will be copied and originals returned.

In complying with this request, you will render a service to Mr. Carnegie's family and friends and greatly facilitate my work. May I hope to hear from you at a reasonably early date?

Very sincerely yours,
Burton J. Hendrick[127]

• • •

127. Someone with the initials E.C. has answered for Van Dyke and written a note to him across the bottom: "Ans. saying you were in the Canal Zone, E.C." Extensive research has failed to uncover the identity of E.C. While Van Dyke himself edited the autobiography of Andrew Carnegie, it is generally held that Hendrick's *Life of Andrew Carnegie* is the first substantive biography. The volume accords the industrialist gentle treatment.

THE NEW YORK WORLD
Editorial Rooms
Mr. Lyman
Rm 414

*April 19, 1927*

Dr. John C. Van Dyke
Librarian
The Sage Library
New Brunswick, N.J.

Dear Mr. Van Dyke:

Apropos of your letter to me from Ancon, and my answer to you on the 8th, I beg to say I have just received a letter from Mr. George Kelly, State Historian, Phoenix, Arizona, in which he says:

> According to accepted authority, Arizona is derived from Arizonac, so-called by the Papago and Pima Indians—the two languages being practically the same—and means "Little Spring." This state was called by the name Arizona by the Spaniards at least as early as 1736 and must have been known to the Indians by their name of Arizonac for probably many years prior to that date: no one may say.
>
> "Ari" means small, and "zonac" means spring.[128]

With best wishes, believe me,

Very truly yours,
R. H. Lyman

[penciled in by Van Dyke:] Ed. of *World Almanac*

• • •

128. Recent scholarship generally agrees with this origin of the state's name (Granger xv). In *The Desert*, Van Dyke tumbles into yet another factual gaffe of his own making by insisting with some heat that Arizona is derived from the Spanish *arida zona* (208). He also mocks those etymologists who disagree with him (208 n). One can only wonder why, after twenty-six years, he was worrying the issue, unless he was still searching for some authority to agree with his original declaration on the matter.

2045 De Mille Drive
Hollywood, California
Phone No. 12733

*May 19 [1927?]*[129]

Dear Van Dyke:

What happened to you? We kept expecting to hear from you, and no word came. Did you go off to Kamchatka or Timbuctoo? I hope this finds you at home. Have you read Van Wyck Brooks' *Emerson?* It seems to me to make Brooks an eligible for the Academy. It is a fine piece of work. He is a true man of letters, far removed from the slap-dash newspaper men around him. Think of it.

I shall be in Onteora in July and August.[130] Zulime will not go east with me. She is much better than when you were here, but that tremor in her hand is at times so strong that she will not meet strangers. Part of the time it is quiescent, and she seems quite all right. She is otherwise vigorous, but she is in doubt about the altitude of Onteora. She wants to go, but the doctors are against the long ride. As she seems likely not to be able to live at Onteora, I am offering Gray Ledge for sale. If any of your friends would be interested, I will make a very low price for the house, car, stock in the club, and for most of the furniture. Some of it I shall ship out here. I shall stay East till my third volume is out of the press, probably till October Fifteenth.

Let's have a word from you.

Faithfully,
H. G.

Hamlin Garland

• • •

129. Though Garland gives no year for this letter, Van Wyck Brooks's *Emerson*, mentioned in the first paragraph, appeared in 1927.

130. Longtime friends and fellow clubmen, Van Dyke and novelist Hamlin Garland owned neighboring "cottages" in the hilly woods of the Catskill's exclusive Onteora Club. See location map in Gaillard (20–21). Photos of the two summer homes also appear in Gaillard: Van Dyke's on 17 and 22, and Garland's truly massive establishment on 19 and 28.

*May 19 [1931?]*

Dear Mr. Van Dyke,

Many thanks for sending me the pamphlet about the Library. I should have found it interesting even if I had not known the place, but as I remember it so well and with such grateful feelings, I have been, of course, doubly interested. It was the chief attractive feature of my stay in New Brunswick, barring, of course, a few people—not many! And after I left there it was very long before I was reconciled to doing without such a place of refuge and entertainment. Even after I came back to New York, where there are certainly many libraries, there was none which did anything like the friendly service of the Sage. And I am grateful not only for the pamphlet but for the very nice compliment you pay me on one of its pages.

I wish that I might see you some time. I hesitate to ask anyone from out of town, or even from far uptown, to come here at any definite time, fearing the exertion would not be paid for by anything I can offer nowadays—nowadays when the conversation of more than two people at a time tires me greatly. But if at any time you find it convenient to come, and will telephone me, I shall gladly be at home at any afternoon you say. I seldom have an engagement that cannot be readily broken. Always,

Sincerely yours,
M. G. Van Rensselaer[131]

• • •

131. Art critic and historian Mrs. Schuyler Van Rensselaer (Mariana Griswold, 1851–1934) lived in New Brunswick from around 1873 to 1884, then moved to New York City. In his *Autobiography* Van Dyke mentions her appreciatively as his early mentor in cultural matters (50–51). The pamphlet referred to in the letter is Van Dyke's *The Sage Library* (1931). This refers to Mrs. Van Rensselaer as a frequent library visitor in the past and now "well known as a writer on art and the author of the best history of New York ever published" (9).

*Ars Gratia Artis*
Metro-Goldwyn-Mayer Studios
Culver City, California

*May 24th, 1932*

Dr. John C. Van Dyke
Theological Seminary
Sage Library
New Brunswick, New Jersey

My Dear Uncle Jack:

I'm off again! This time to the Arctic and will winter in [illegible word] headquarters in Point Barrow. Letters addressed to Metro-Goldwyn-Mayer, Point Barrow, will eventually reach me, as I will have a plane coming to take out film once every seven or eight weeks.

Am going to film Peter Freuchen's book *Eskimo.* Don't fancy the job a damn bit, but it brings in the bread and butter.

Don't know where this is apt to reach you, but where you are, good luck and good health.

Woody

[penciled in by Van Dyke:] W. S. Van Dyke, movie director of *Trader Horn*, *Tarzan the Ape Man*, *White Shadows of the South Sea*, etc.[132]

• • •

132. Cannom offers a biography of well-known movie director Woodbridge (Woody) Strong Van Dyke.

# *Selected Bibliography*

Abbey, Edward. *Desert Solitaire: A Season in the Wilderness.* New York: McGraw-Hill, 1968.

Aitken, William Benford. *Distinguished Families in America Descended from Wilhelmus Beekman and Jan Thomasse Van Dyke.* New York: Knickerbocker, 1912.

Almada, Francisco R. *Diccionario de historia, geografía y biografía sonorenses.* 1952. Hermosillo [Mexico]: Instituto Sonorense de Cultura, 1950.

Amdur, Mary O., John Doull, and Curtis D. Klaassen, eds. *Casarett and Doull's Toxicology: The Basic Science of Poisons.* 4th ed. New York: Pergamon Press, 1991.

Aronson, Marc. "Wharton and the House of Scribner: The Novelist as a Pain in the Neck." *New York Times Book Review,* January 2, 1994, 7–8.

Ayer, Edward Everett. "Second Part of Mr. Ayer's Journal for 1918." 26 pp. typescript (carbon). From the "Reminiscences." Courtesy the Edward Everett Ayer Papers, The Newberry Library Archives, The Newberry Library, Chicago.

Bailey, Anthony. "The Art World: A Young Man on Horseback." *New Yorker,* March 5, 1990, 45–48, 50–53, 56–77.

Ballinger, James K. *Frederic Remington's Southwest.* Phoenix: Phoenix Art Museum, 1992.

Bates, Ernest Sutherland. "Brownell, William Crary." In *Dictionary of*

*American Biography*, edited by Dumas Malone. Vol. 3. New York: Charles Scribner's Sons, 1946.

Bell, Millicent. *Edith Wharton and Henry James: The Story of Their Friendship.* New York: George Braziller, 1965.

Browne, J. Ross. *Adventures in the Apache Country: A Tour through Arizona and Sonora, with Notes on the Silver Regions of Nevada.* New York: Harper, 1869.

Buck, Wendy, and Peter Wild. "Viewing America's Deserts, Part V. Two Desert Radicals: Mary Austin and her 'Mentor.'" *Puerto del Sol* 31, no. 2 (summer 1996): 258–76.

Cable, Mary. *Top Drawer: American High Society from the Gilded Age to the Roaring Twenties.* New York: Atheneum, 1984.

Cannom, Robert C. *Van Dyke and the Mythical City, Hollywood.* Culver City: Murray and Gee, 1948.

Carnegie, Andrew. *Autobiography of Andrew Carnegie.* Edited by John C. Van Dyke. Boston: Houghton Mifflin, 1920.

Carr, Harry. "Mrs. Wells' Gold Spike Unites Salt Lake Lines." *Los Angeles Times*, January 31, 1905, 1.

———. "Ready-Made Towns Dumped Off Trains." *Los Angeles Times*, February 2, 1905, editorial sec., 1, 6.

———. "Wolves on Desert after Greek's Cash." *Los Angeles Times*, February 1, 1905, 1.

"Coronation Exhibition." *Times* (London), May 1, 1911, 7.

"Countess Mercati, Patron of the Arts." *New York Times*, February 5, 1951, 23.

"Crane, Bruce." In *Encyclopedia of American Art.* New York: E. P. Dutton, 1981.

Demarest, David P., Jr. Afterword to *The Homestead Strike of 1892*, by Arthur G. Burgoyne. 1893. Reprint, Pittsburgh: University of Pittsburgh Press, 1979.

Gaillard, E. Davis. *Onteora: Hills of the Sky, 1887–1987.* [Tannersville: Onteora Club,] 1987.

Garland, Hamlin. *Afternoon Neighbors: Further Excerpts from a Literary Log.* New York: Macmillan, 1934. Pp. 117–18.

———. *Hamlin Garland's Diaries*, edited by Donald Pizer. San Marino: Huntington Library, 1968. Pp. 62, 227–28.

———. "John Charles Van Dyke." In *Commemorative Tributes of the American Academy of Arts and Letters, 1905–1941.* New York: American Academy of Arts and Letters, 1942. Pp. 291–93.

Granger, Byrd H. *Will C. Barnes' Arizona Place Names.* Tucson: University of Arizona Press, 1960.

Guérard, Albert. *Art for Art's Sake.* Boston: Lothrop, Lee, and Shepard, 1936.

Hacker, Louis M. *The World of Andrew Carnegie, 1865–1901.* Philadelphia: J. B. Lippincott, 1968.

Hellman, Geoffrey T. "Some Splendid and Admirable People." *New Yorker,* February 23, 1976, 43–48, 52–54, 60–64, 68–81.

Hendrick, Burton J. *The Life of Andrew Carnegie.* 2 vols. Garden City: Doubleday, 1932.

Ingham, Zita, and Peter Wild. "The Preface as Illumination: The Curious (If Not Tricky) Case of John C. Van Dyke's *The Desert.*" *Rhetoric Review* 9 (1991): 328–39.

James, George Wharton. *The Wonders of the Colorado Desert.* 2 vols. Boston: Little, Brown, 1906.

Ladies' Depository. *Annual Report* [1847]. New York: The Depository, 1847.

Langlois, Karen S. "Mary Austin and Houghton Mifflin Company: A Case Study in the Marketing of a Western Writer." *Western American Literature* 23, no. 1 (spring 1988): 31–42.

Lee, W. Storrs. *The Great California Deserts.* New York: Putnam's, 1963.

Leonard, William Ellery. *Two Lives.* New York: Viking Press, 1925.

Lewis, R. W. B. *Edith Wharton: A Biography.* New York: Harper and Row, 1975.

Lindsay, Vachel. *Collected Poems.* New York: Macmillan, 1925.

Lochman, Katharine A. *The Etchings of James McNeill Whistler.* New Haven: Yale University Press, 1984.

Loti, Pierre. *The Desert.* Translated by Jay Paul Minn. Salt Lake City: University of Utah Press, 1993. Originally published as *Le Désert* (Paris: Calmann-Lévy, 1895).

Mather, Frank Jewett, Jr. "Van Dyke, John Charles." In *Dictionary of American Biography,* edited by Dumas Malone. Vol. 10. New York: Charles Scribner's Sons, 1946.

Matthews, James Brander. "Glad Nights and Days under the Blue Sky." Review of *The Open Spaces,* by John C. Van Dyke. *New York Times Book Review,* May 7, 1922, 3.

Morris, Harrison S. "The Art Collection of John G. Johnson." *Scribner's Magazine* 68, no. 3 (September 1920): 379–84.

———. *Confessions in Art.* New York: Sears, 1930.

———. *Hannah Bye.* Philadelphia: Penn, 1920.

———. *Lyrics and Landscapes.* New York: Century, 1908.

———. *Martial Notes of the Old War and the New.* Philadelphia: Lippincott, 1929.

———. *Masterpieces of the Sea. William T. Richards: A Brief Outline of His Life and Art.* Philadelphia: Lippincott, 1912.

Nash, Roderick. *Wilderness and the American Mind.* 3d ed. New Haven: Yale University Press, 1982.

"Pan-American Unity Urged." *New York Times,* November 12, 1930, 47.

Parr, Clare Van Dyke Lambert. "Last Will and Testament of Clare Van Dyke Lambert Parr." Dated May 5, 1952. Proved December 10, 1963. Surrogate's Court of Westchester County, White Plains, New York.

Pennell, Joseph. *The Adventures of an Illustrator: Mostly in Following His Authors in America and Europe.* Boston: Little, Brown, 1925.

———. *The Graphic Arts: Modern Men and Modern Methods.* The Scammon Lectures for 1920. Chicago: University of Chicago Press, 1921.

Pisano, Ronald G. *Idle Hours: Americans at Leisure, 1865–1914.* Boston: Little, Brown, 1988.

———. *William Merritt Chase.* New York: Watson-Guptill, 1979.

Powell, Lawrence Clark. *Southwest Classics: The Creative Literature of the Arid Lands.* 1974. Reprint, Tucson: University of Arizona Press, 1982.

"Prof. J. C. Van Dyke, Art Authority, Dies." *New York Times,* December 6, 1932, 21.

*San Miguel de Horcacitas, H 12, D 31, Sonora.* Map. México, D.F. [Mexico]: Comisión de Estudios del Territorio Nacional, 1973.

Strong, Philip L. Foreword to *The Autobiography of John C. Van Dyke: A Personal Narrative of American Life, 1861–1931,* by John C. Van Dyke. Edited by Peter Wild. Salt Lake City: University of Utah Press, 1993.

Sullivan, John B., Jr., and Gary R. Krieger, eds. *Hazardous Materials Toxicology: Clinical Principles of Environmental Health.* Baltimore: Williams and Wilkins, 1992.

Teague, David. "A Paradoxical Legacy: Some New Contexts for John C. Van Dyke's *The Desert.*" *Western American Literature* 30, no. 2 (summer 1995): 163–78.

———. "A Sometime Ruskinite in the Wilderness: John C. Van Dyke's Desert Aesthetic." *Southwestern American Literature* 21, no. 1 (fall 1995): 221–25.

Teague, David, and Peter Wild. "The Secret Life of John C. Van Dyke: Decalcomania on the Desert." *Journal of the Southwest* 37, no. 1 (spring 1995): 1–52.

Van Dyke, Dix. *Daggett: Life in a Mojave Frontier Town.* Edited by Peter Wild. Baltimore: Johns Hopkins University Press. Forthcoming book edition of "Reminiscenses of Daggett" (below).

———. "Law on the Desert." *Westways* 29, no. 11 (1937): 14–16.

———. "Old Times in Daggett." *Westways* 35, no. 2, pt. 1 (1943): 16–17.

———. "Reminiscences of Daggett." A manuscript printed under various titles, such as "The Pioneer Story" and "Pioneers"; the selections appear in a long series of articles published on intermittent Thursdays in the *Barstow (California) Printer Review* from April through December 1953, the year after Dix's death. A partial and variant onionskin typescript of the series is in the holdings of the Mojave River Valley Museum, Barstow, California.

Van Dyke, John C. *American Painting and Its Tradition.* New York: Charles Scribner's Sons, 1910.

———. *Art for Art's Sake: Seven University Lectures on the Technical Beauties of Painting.* New York: Charles Scribner's Sons, 1914.

———. *The Autobiography of John C. Van Dyke: A Personal Narrative of American Life, 1861–1931.* Edited by Peter Wild. Salt Lake City: University of Utah Press, 1993.

———. *The Desert: Further Studies in Natural Appearances.* New York: Charles Scribner's Sons, 1901. Reprint, with an introduction by Richard Shelton, Salt Lake City: Peregrine Smith, 1980.

———. *The Desert: Further Studies in Natural Appearances.* Photographs by J. Smeaton Chase. New York: Charles Scribner's Sons, 1918.

———. *The Grand Canyon of the Colorado: Recurrent Studies in Impressions and Appearances.* New York: Charles Scribner's Sons, 1920. Reprint, with an introduction by Peter Wild, Salt Lake City: University of Utah Press, 1992.

———. *How to Judge of a Picture: Familiar Talks in the Gallery with Uncritical Lovers of Art.* New York: Chautauqua, 1888.

———. *In the West Indies: Sketches and Studies in Tropic Seas and Islands.* New York: Charles Scribner's Sons, 1932.

———. "Lincoln's Reading and Modesty." *Century Magazine* 81, no. 4 (February 1911): 597–98.

———. "The Lotto Portrait of Columbus." *Century Magazine* 44 (October 1892): 818–22; reproduction of portrait on 802.

———. *The Meadows: Familiar Studies of the Commonplace.* New York: Charles Scribner's Sons, 1926.

———. *The Money God: Chapters of Heresy and Dissent Concerning Business Methods and Mercenary Ideals in American Life.* New York: Charles Scribner's Sons, 1908.

———. *The Mountain: Renewed Studies in Impressions and Appearances.* New York: Charles Scribner's Sons, 1916. Reprint, with an introduction by Peter Wild, Salt Lake City: University of Utah Press, 1992.

———. *Nature for Its Own Sake: First Studies in Natural Appearances.* New York: Charles Scribner's Sons, 1898.

———. *The New New York: A Commentary on the Place and the People.* Illustrations by Joseph Pennell. New York: Charles Scribner's Sons, 1909.

———. *Old English Masters, Engraved by Timothy Cole.* New York: Century, 1902.

———. *The Opal Sea: Continued Studies in Impressions and Appearances.* New York: Charles Scribner's Sons, 1906.

———. *The Open Spaces: Incidents of Nights and Days under the Blue Sky.* New York: Charles Scribner's Sons, 1922. Reprint, with an introduction by Peter Wild, Salt Lake City: University of Utah Press, 1991.

———. "Painting at the Fair." *Century Magazine* 48, no. 26 (July 1994): 439–47.

———. *Principles of Art.* New York: Fords, Howard, and Hulbert, 1887.

———. *The Raritan: Notes on a River and a Family.* New Brunswick: privately printed, 1915.

———. *Rembrandt and His School: A Critical Study of the Master and His Pupils, with a New Assignment of Their Pictures.* New York: Charles Scribner's Sons, 1923.

———. *The Rembrandt Drawings and Etchings, with Critical Reassignments to Pupils and Followers.* New York: Charles Scribner's Sons, 1927.

———. *The Sage Library: Its Books, Manuscripts and Portraits.* Special issue of *New Brunswick Seminary Bulletin* 6, no. 1 (1931): 1–34.

———. *The Story of the Pine.* New York: Authors Club, 1893.

———. *What Is Art?: Studies in the Technique and Criticism of Painting.* New York: Charles Scribner's Sons, 1910.

Van Rensselaer, M[ariana] G[riswold]. "Pictures of the Season in New York, II." *American Architect and Building News* 19 (February 27, 1886): 104.

Walker, Franklin. *A Literary History of Southern California.* Berkeley: University of California Press, 1950.

Wall, John P. *Chronicles of New Brunswick, New Jersey, 1667–1931.* New Brunswick: privately printed, 1931.

Wharton, Edith. *The House of Mirth.* New York: Charles Scribner's Sons, 1905. Reprint, New York: Oxford University Press, 1994.

Wild, Peter. "How a London Madman Painted Our Deserts." *North Dakota Quarterly* 63, no. 2 (spring 1996): 5–17.

———. "Interviews and Notes Regarding John C. Van Dyke." Archives of the American Academy of Arts and Letters and of the University of Arizona Library. Sealed until 2009.

———. *John C. Van Dyke: The Desert.* Boise: Boise State University, 1988.

———. "John Muir and the Desert Connection." *John Muir Newsletter* 5, no. 2 (spring 1995): 2, 6.

———. "John Muir and the Van Dyke Ranch: Intimacy and Desire in His Final Years, Part 1." *John Muir Newsletter* 5, no. 3 (summer 1995): 1, 4–5.

———. "John Muir and the Van Dyke Ranch: Intimacy and Desire in His Final Years, Part 2." *John Muir Newsletter* 5, no. 4 (fall 1995): 1, 3-5, 6.

———. *Theodore Strong Van Dyke.* Boise: Boise State University, 1995. Western Writers Series #121.

———. "Viewing America's Deserts, Part 1: John C. Van Dyke and the French Connection." *Puerto del Sol* 26, no. 2 (1991): 58–78.

———. "A Western Sun Sets in the East: The Five 'Appearances' Surrounding John C. Van Dyke's *The Desert.*" *Western American Literature* 25 (1990): 218–31.

———. "A Writer in a Wild Frontier Town: The Contribution of Theodore Strong Van Dyke." *South Dakota Review* 32, no. 3 (fall 1994): 51–64.

Wild, Peter, and Neil Carmony. "The Trip Not Taken." *Journal of Arizona History* 34, no. 1 (1993): 65–80.

Wilhelm, Donald. "A Lumberman Bibliophile." *Outlook* 110, no. 17 (August 25, 1915): 997–1001.

Wolfe, Linnie Marsh. *Son of the Wilderness: The Life of John Muir.* New York: Knopf, 1945. Pp. 309–10, 327, 347–48.

# *Index*

References to illustrations are printed in italics.

# *About the Editors*

David W. Teague is assistant professor of English in the University of Delaware Parallel Program. He is the author of *The Southwest in American Literature and Art: The Rise of a Desert Aesthetic.* Teague received his Ph.D. in English from the University of Virginia; he serves as secretary for the Association for the Study of Literature and Environment.

Peter Wild is professor of English at the University of Arizona and the author or editor of forty books. He is also a poet, journalist, backpacker, and conservationist. Wild has contributed articles to numerous magazines and journals, including *Smithsonian*, *Sierra*, and *The New York Times Book Review.*